Self-Publish
The Easy Way

Self-Publish
The Easy Way

*How to Work with the
Professionals You Need*

Michael Rohani

NEXT*f*OLIO®

Self-Publish the Easy Way: How to Work with the Professionals You Need

Library of Congress Control Number: 2009903530
ISBN-10: 0-9816771-0-X
ISBN-13: 978-0-9816771-0-1

Printed in the United States of America.

Cover and interior design: DesignForBooks.com
Copy editing: Kathleen Erickson and Michelle Goodman

DISCLAIMER
This book is intended to provide authoritative information with regard to self-publishing. It is sold with the understanding that the publisher and author are not engaged in rendering legal or other professional services. For any legal advice required, always seek the services of a competent legal professional. The concepts and services explained in this book are for informational purposes only. The examples and advice provided in this book should not to be construed to guaranty economic success. You must use your own independent judgment as to the viability and risks of any business transaction. There are many variables that determine the success or failure of book products. Following the advice given in this book does not guaranty that you will publish books profitably or avoid suffering losses.

WWW.NEXTFOLIO.COM

Contents

Introduction

Self-publish for fun, for profit, to promote your business, to enhance your credentials, to spread your ideas, to share your creativity—this book is the concise guide to publishing for authors and businesses wanting to self-publish without doing all the work themselves.

In particular, this book is for authors who want the same high standards and quality found among books published by professional publishers. That is the level of quality necessary, for example, to encourage a reviewer to write a positive review, to get a bookstore to stock the book, and most of all, to be attractive to the book buyer. This book is for you if you want that kind of quality—either because you intend to compete in the marketplace or because you care enough about your book to have it produced in the best way. In the following chapters, I will explain why it is that most self-published books fail and what you can do to avoid the same fate. I'll also explain what you can do during each of the main stages of publishing to make the process go smoothly and to

> **Tip** Understanding how publishers work with industry professionals to create quality books will enable you to get the services you really need and to avoid wasting time and money.

get the results you require for success.

You'll learn what types of professionals to hire, how to determine their level of expertise, how to speak their jargon, and how to best ensure they complete the job to your satisfaction. You'll learn how to avoid common mistakes, how to cut costs without sacrificing quality, and which printing technologies to use and when. Successful publishing requires skill and hard work, and the secret to self-publishing the easy way is getting the right professionals to do the hard work for you.

In *Self-Publish the Easy Way* you'll learn all the publication essentials from manuscript preparation up through actual publication. Book marketing is such an important topic of its own, that I have devoted a separate book to it. *Book Marketing Essentials*, explains how to develop and manage effective marketing strategies—and much more. That said, marketing is so important that I have also included many important marketing tips in *Self-Publish the Easy Way*, too.

A self-publishing revolution is now under way. With every passing day, it is becoming easier and more affordable to self-publish, but it is also easier to get scammed or to produce a book that will never sell. The challenge facing authors is how to cut costs when self-publishing, but without cutting out the quality required to be successful.

The percentage of books being self-published is every year rising dramatically, and more new businesses are coming online to profit from authors. Some of these businesses make extraordinary claims and offer amazingly low prices for all sorts of services. Aspects of these services can sometimes be worthwhile, but some are too far below industry standards to be useful. It isn't always the case that you get what you pay for—sometimes you pay and pretty much get nothing. As a consumer, knowledge is always your best defense against spending money for services that are inadequate, unnecessary, or useless.

The more you know about the publishing business and how professionals work together to create quality books, the more you will be able to find the services you really need and to avoid wasting time and money. Promises that sound too good to be true—such as the promise that a simple barcode will give you access to thousands of retailers—are so seductive that wishful authors can fail to see the obvious. The simple fact is that many thousands of books are self-published every week, most by print-on-demand companies, and these books are not showing up in retail bookshops. It takes more than simply meeting a retail requirement, such as acquiring an ISBN or barcode, to create an attractive book that distributors actually want.

Your chances of getting real distribution are far greater if you produce a quality book that people want. The key to producing any quality product is getting skilled industry professionals to do the work for you—the same talented people used by publishers. *Despite the claims of some self-publishing advocates, producing a quality book and marketing it successfully actually involves diverse and specialized skills.*

Let me put this a different way—there are lots of companies that are set up to make money from authors without doing anything that will necessarily make money for authors. Experienced publishers rarely use these services. If you want your book done right, do what real publishers do. How that's done is what I'll explain in this book.

Tip There are lots of companies that are set up to make money from authors without providing any-thing that will likely make money for the authors.

In this book, I'll tell you what kinds of professionals you need to hire and what you need to know when working with them. Unlike other self-publishing books, I will not attempt, or pretend, to teach you the many skills involved in professional book production, rather I will give you the insider information and terminology you need to know to work efficiently and successfully with professionals who do have the skills to do the work for you—and to do it the right way. Unlike other books on self-publishing, this book is not a do-everything-yourself guide to producing an amateur book product. This book is for authors wise enough to know their real strengths and weaknesses and who are aware that they are unlikely to match the expertise of professionals who acquired their experience while serving the book industry—the industry that is responsible for the books that actually do get into the bookshops. A successful author will have better things to do than to try to master all these difficult professional publishing skills anyway.

Self-publishing does not have to be hugely expensive, but if you are going to spend any money on professional services, then it makes sense to learn what you can about quality standards and industry safeguards to protect your investment. Quality will almost always cost some money, and it is that cost that is the main reason publishers established standards and procedures for what they do. If your goal is to ensure that your hard work of writing a book is not wasted because the end result is unprofessional and unattractive to consumers, then you can use the information in this book.

Why Self-publish?

Everyone who wants to be published should consider self-publishing simply because successful self-publishing usually increases, rather than decreases, your chances of getting a major publisher to carry your book. That is, if you self-publish and then later decide to consider a publisher, you still can. That said, the two main reasons many authors choose to self-publish are 1) their subject matter is not of interest to publishers (i.e., they must self-publish) or 2) because self-publishing increases the likelihood of making a much greater profit.

After the publisher and distributors take their cut, author royalties are usually too small to make writing worthwhile financially. This is true for the vast majority of authors. Whereas an author who self-publishes can sometimes cover all his or her costs and start making a profit after the first thousand books have been sold. This is especially true for authors who have the means to distribute books directly through their own business, personal connections, or the Internet.

Self-publishing has been around for a long time. In fact, the English poet John Milton published a book about it in 1644. Nevertheless, self-publishing remained too costly for most people until recently. New technologies have made it more affordable than at any time in history. The result of these changes has brought about an explosion of self-publishing. This growth in self-publishing also corresponds with a decline in the number of new books being published by traditional publishers.

With the declining chance of being published by a traditional publisher, authors can find encouragement in the facts that 1) there are more and more readers searching for new books on topics and material that no one in the past would have considered and that 2) there are fewer obstacles to preserving and distributing in some form of publication one's own stories, interesting ideas, "how-to" expertise, technical information, or family history, etc. Publishing has changed dramatically in the last few decades, and the range of what people find interesting and useful to read is likewise changing. With the Internet, people can find most anything without going to a bookstore.

Even so, self-publishing remains problematic for most authors. The most notable difficulty with self-publishing is marketplace visibility. That is, most authors lack any means of effective distribution and their books are simply never seen. When you do see them, there are other serious problems. Most self-published books are ugly and put together badly. This is the main reason that distributors and stores reject them. It's enough to say that a book looks self-published for people to understand that you mean amateurish. The unprofessional appearance is seen as an early warning sign of greater problems inside the book, such as poor editing, tangential information, and incomprehensible content.

When you pick up a book published by a professional trade publisher, you assume that the book has been carefully vetted and edited, that it has been designed and typeset correctly, and that it has had the benefit of extensive marketing. None of this is necessarily true, but it is more likely to be true with a professional publisher than with a self-published author. This is because publishers avoid books that lack commercial merit. A book must warrant the financial risks involved in hiring editors, designers, and especially printers.

Publishers rely on teams of paid experts, and they have powerful marketing channels that are often closed to self-publishing authors. In the past, it was hard for authors to find the right book professionals. Companies that promise to provide these services to authors in package deals rarely do so at a quality level comparable to what publishers expect. Given the problems involved in self-publishing and the obvious advantages publishers have, why should anyone attempt it, even with the new innovations of the last decade?

As I will explain in the next chapter, your choice does not have to be between getting a quality book through a traditional publisher relationship or getting a poorly put together self-published book because you did it yourself. However, for the moment, let's set aside the question of quality and look more at good reasons why some authors either prefer to self-publish or do so when they simply must self-publish.

THE BENEFITS OF SELF-PUBLISHING

If a person, business, or institution has the right credentials for the book's topic and can get a good agent who can put the book into the hands of a publisher willing to publish it, there are still six main reasons to self-publish anyway.

1 **Editorial control:** Even authors who are humble and wise enough to submit to much-needed editing find that some publishers simply want to take too much editorial license. They may, in fact, cut out the main substance of the book or change the entire perspective on the topic. Some publishers cut costs by eliminating careful editing and proofing altogether. Publishers don't just edit, they concept-edit books to make them fit in with their other published material and to fit in with their own marketing strategies and budget. The publisher's editorial control isn't just about grammar and punctuation, it's about the content, length, appearance, and even the presentation of the final product.

2 **Design control:** Many publishers never involve the author in the design of the book, only allowing them to see it once it's completed. Publishers usually stipulate in the "standard" contract that the publisher—not the author—has the final say in how the book looks. They decide how much effort and expense will go into the production of each book. Your dream of the great cover image or color interior may never happen. The book's design and presentation can directly affect the public's perception of you and your book's credibility and value.

3 **Ownership:** Many publisher contracts will take the copyright from the author, meaning that the author loses pretty much everything except the promise of a royalty check, which may or may not materialize. In this situation, the author may lose all control over the content of the book and never likely get the book back under their own control no matter how well or how bad the publisher is at selling it. Some publisher contracts leave the copyright ownership in the hands of the author—the rightful creator—but establish a "license" agreement for the *duration of the copyright.* Written this way, it is pretty much the same as taking away the copyright, because the duration of the copyright extends seventy years past the life of the author. The only way out is to die and wait seventy years!

Some savvy and/or already established authors may be successful in negotiating some sort of automatic termination or performance clause that will give the author the option to recover the book (to publish themselves or to take to another publisher) after a certain number of years or after the publisher can no longer sell it effectively. However, many publishers will have reasons to refuse to agree to such terms. Normally, an author has to hope the publisher will be really good at selling the book—i.e., there is so much money from the royalties that the effective loss of control and ownership is not so onerous.

It's a sad fact that the vast majority of authors, once they license a book to the wrong publisher, are unlikely to be able to get it back so that they can give it to a better publisher. And, what's more, some publishers reserve the right to sell off the title to whomsoever they want, whenever they want.

4 **Your future as an author:** Standard publishers' contracts often contain a clause that restricts what an author can publish in any future books. Typically the clause will restrict an author's ability to publish any other work that the publisher believes, in their judgment, may compete

with the book they have already published. This may at first sound reasonable, but if you plan to write more books in your line of expertise and experience, but your publisher isn't interested in publishing them, then agreeing to such a clause could effectively be the kiss of death to your future as an author. Self-publishing is one way to eliminate this risk altogether.

5 **Higher profits:** Typically, an author makes only about 7% net from the sale of a book. *Net* sales is the actual profit from the book after discounts and other cuts, such as distributor cuts—that is, much less than 7% of the cover price. Let's say, for example, you spend a year writing a book and a publisher publishes it. The cover price is $20 and we'll assume for calculation purposes that the publisher has agreed to a generous 7% *gloss* of the actualy cover price. The publisher prints and sells 10,000 copies over a period of four years and then backlists the book, selling only a few copies per year after that (the print run will likely be closer to 4,000 books or fewer). The distributors take 50% of the cover price. The publisher is then left with the remaining 50%, of which the author gets 7%. This 7% return would average only $1,750 per year for the course of the four years. In comparison, the total return on the same quantity self-published and sold directly by the author at the full cover price is $200,000. This is why some publishers do

> **Tip** It's possible to make far more money from self-publishing than from publisher royalties.

short print runs for most new titles. It minimizes risks, and in the end, unlike the author, they can still make a worthwhile profit. Publishers need a certain number of books per year to satisfy their distributors, and they will therefore include some titles even if they don't intend to print very many copies or to spend much to market them. Getting published by an established publisher is no guarantee that your book will receive the attention and effort you could afford to give it if you were the one profiting from it.

6 You can self-publish and still publish again with a publisher: It becomes much easier to publish with a good publisher if you have already self-published successfully. When an author shows the receipts—i.e., proves market demand for a book—a publisher can see the value of the book. Richard Evans was unable to find a publisher for his children's book, *The Christmas Box*, so he self-published it in 1993 and distributed it to bookstores in his community. It became a local bestseller. When it made it to *The New York Times* bestseller's list a few years later, he signed with Simon & Schuster, who paid him $4.2 million in advance.

> **Tip** Self-publishing can be an alternative to using a publisher, or a prelude to it.

Self-publishing can be an alternative to using a publisher, OR, a prelude to it.Increasingly, publishers are only interested in authors who can show that they can market their own book. They want to know if an author is, for example, already doing readings, workshops, or seminars. But if authors can market their own book themselves anyway, it makes more sense for them to get as much money from their own marketing efforts before signing up with publishers who do have some larger marketing channels unavailable to authors. Once a publisher has reached the limits of its own sales capabilities, the book is often sold to another publisher who re-packages it for its own market. Self-published authors can do the same thing. Once an author reaches the limits of his or her own ability to sell a book, then it is a good time to look for a publisher who has access to new markets.

AUTHORS WHO MUST SELF-PUBLISH

You may be an author who can get a publisher, but for the six reasons listed above, know that it's better to go solo. However, there are some authors who can never get a good publisher. These authors simply have to self-publish. Why? There are two basic reasons:

1 **The author problem:** Some authors are unknown and lack the formal credentials to convince a publisher to take them seriously. For example, if you are writing about architecture, psychology, politics, etc., but you don't teach the subject at a major university or even have a degree in the field, then you will be viewed as lacking sufficient credentials.

In some cases you may have the credentials, but the problem may be as simple as not already being a published author or not having an agent. Large publishers receive so many manuscripts that they refuse to even consider them unless they are submitted by a well-established "author agent," and, increasingly, getting a good agent to look at one's manuscript is nearly as difficult as getting in the door of a publisher without an agent. You can try smaller, lesser-known publishers, but if that fails you will be left on your own.

2 **The book problem:** Some books are about obscure or controversial topics that are only of interest to a small number of people. Some books are about topics that have already been written about so many times that the market is saturated with similar books. Publishers are unwilling or reluctant to take on book projects that are difficult to market, are unlikely to generate substantial sales, and are about topics or views they don't want to be associated with or believe may involve them in legal headaches.

SELF-PUBLISHING FOR PROFESSIONAL PRESTIGE AND/OR PERSONAL PLEASURE

In addition to authors who can't get a publisher, but who have books that might sell well if they were self-published, there are some authors who have books that are never likely to do well financially, but are still worth publishing. These books fall into two main categories:

1 **Career and business enhancement books:** Being the author of a book is a way of gaining credibility and prestige and sharing expertise. It can help you and your business. An author is perceived as an authority—one who has "written the book" on the topic. Even when the market is saturated with good books on the same topic, people like knowing that they are talking to someone who is expert enough on a topic to have actually written a book about it. Being an author counts for something! The same is true for businesses. Just as books can promote an individual's credentials, books can help promote business products and services. In some cases, a book's mere existence and appearance can build a company's brand identity and influence transactions. Some books can be so beneficial to a business that it makes more sense to give them away than to sell them. There are books that communicate a company's image, books that reduce sales interaction time and consultation time, books that catalog products and services, and books that communicate important information or answer frequent client questions. There are also businesses, such as restaurants and historical sites, that can sell more books over the counter than many publishers could ever hope to sell. Self-publishing can be a very cost-effective advertising tool or way of creating products.

2 **Books for personal satisfaction:** You may have a story to tell, a history to relate, a scrapbook of interesting family or business artifacts, a photo album, etc., that may only be of interest to a small circle of acquaintances or to their own extended family. Nevertheless, the simple pleasure of writing such a book, or a short forward to a collection of photographs, and seeing it self-published in a credible and professional manner may be enough to justify the costs of producing a limited number of quality books.

Whatever the reason you decided to self-publish, it should never mean that you have to settle for a low-quality book. If you're writing a book simply as a labor of love, then perhaps you will not be as concerned about quality editing, design, or printing. Authors who are self-publishing for career or business enhancement, however, will likely find that it matters to have it done right. Likewise, authors who want to compete in the marketplace for profit need to be concerned with the quality and presentation of their books. In the next chapter, I will explain some realities about book publishing that you must know to prevent your book from becoming a failure like the majority of self-published books are.

2

What You Must Know about Self-publishing

Some people believe that self-publishing means doing all the work yourself, and this is exactly what some self-publishing authors attempt to do. While a do-it-yourself author may feel proud of being able to stick together a book and get it printed, booksellers and consumers are more interested in buying the best book—they are not likely to give an author extra credit for his or her amateur editing and design accomplishments. Some small publishers are not much better. One can attend a publisher's trade show, like that of the American Booksellers Association (ABA), and take a short walk from the trade publishers' to the small publishers' sections and quickly see the difference. Many smaller publishers simply are not willing to invest in design or quality production. And naturally, one cannot avoid suspecting that the editorial content is not much better.

There is really no sane reason for an author to work hard on a project and then see it ruined in the final stages by having it published in a substandard way. If your book is going to compete in the marketplace against the books of successful publishers, then you need to level the playing field by hiring professionals who will do the job right. It makes a difference. It's why successful publishers hire experts, and it's why you should, too.

VANITY PUBLISHING AND PRINT-ON-DEMAND

In the past it was nearly impossible for authors to escape the problem of poor quality if they chose to self-publish. Even if a qualified editor was willing to work directly with an inexperienced author, a good book designer was very hard to find. It was even more difficult to find the production people necessary to turn book designs into properly typeset page layouts that a printer could actually print. All of this has changed with the Internet. It is now possible to locate the professionals you need with very little effort.

In the past, most self-publishing authors felt it necessary to hire companies set up to do these tasks for authors—the so-called "vanity" presses—a whole industry of companies that have long had a bad reputation for providing low-quality services and products for very high fees—fees that were sometimes hidden. It is well-known that the people who profit the most from self-publishing authors are the vanity presses who rarely sell any books. You can think of a vanity press as a project manager who profits from your book regardless of whether it has any inherent quality or ever ends up being sold to anyone.

These companies are notorious for having sales staff to persuade authors to buy expensive services and print unreasonably large quantities of books. No matter how bad your book may be, they will encourage you to invest as much as possible in their services.

Since 2000, some new forms of vanity publishing have appeared online—companies that offer various services to self-publishing authors including print-on-demand technology. They are primarily digital printing companies who generate their revenues by printing books that are bought by the authors themselves. Like vanity presses of the past, they, too, always profit whether or not you, the author, ever sell a copy of your book to anyone else. They also profit from selling low-cost editing and design services, automated production services, distribution services, and setup fees for the digital printing. These companies are often called *subsidy* publishers, meaning you subsidize or pay for the costs of producing your own book. This is unlike traditional publishing, because with the traditional publishing model the publisher covers the costs of editing, design, printing, and marketing. Subsidy publishers are not, however, always easy to identify, because they may call themselves POD publishers or simply publishers. *POD* means *print-on-demand*, and only refers to the type of printing used, not to a publishing model.

There are two main difficulties with subsidy publishers or POD publishers:

- **Poor credibility:** Most subsidy or POD publishers issue the ISBN for the author's book, and this means that the subsidy or POD publisher is identified on record as the publisher. This is a problem because these companies have a bad reputation with the book trade, meaning the book distributors, book reviewers, and book retailers. Anyone who looks up the book and sees that your book is published by a well-known subsidy publisher is likely to avoid the book like some infectious disease. This is because they know these companies don't screen or vet what they publish. They assume the book was not good enough to be published by a real publisher. (If you self-publish using your own publisher name and get your own ISBN, you may not have a reputation, but at least you don't have a bad one!)

- **Bad publishing economics:** POD books cost too much per copy to compete with offset or process printed books. POD printing gives you lower startup costs because you can print as few copies as you like— in fact, as few as one copy of your book—but the actual *unit costs* (total costs per book) is much higher than offset or process printing, and it is therefore very hard for authors to make any profit from their books if they ever do get more distribution. Bookstores want 40– 50% of the cover price and that means a book must be printed cheaply to be profitable. A POD book may cost $8–9 to print. If you print books to show around to bookstores, what's the point if the cover price is going to be about $16? There is no profit, and if you raise the price, who would buy it when there are so many alternative books by established publishers? This is the second reason why you'll rarely if ever see a POD book in a bookshop.

With POD books, the editing, the design (usually one basic template used for many different kinds of books), the prepress production, and the printing quality all fall short of the industry standards upheld by traditional publishers.

The more complicated the book (such as with how-to books), the more difficult it becomes to use these services to produce the book you need. Very few authors who use these services ever sell more than a few books. Millions of books have been

Tip For many authors, the best use for print-on-demand is for advance publicity and market testing.

"published" in this manner. Some bookstores simply will not order print-on-demand books because these books are more likely to have print quality problems too that will lead to higher return rates (low sales).

Another difficulty with *some* print-on-demand publishing services is that once you purchase their design services, you can't take back your book. You can take back the words, but not the designed files you bought and used to print the book. If you are ready to print your book using a different company, or yourself with a higher quality offset printer, you must start over and pay someone else to create new files for you. Your original startup investment is lost.

When these services sell an ISBN to an author, you need to be aware that these numbers are likewise not released to the author if the author wants to take the book to someone else—they belong to the publisher. The number is only for their edition of the book. Even though you are supposedly "self-publishing" with some of these print-on-demand companies, you do not have the control that normally comes from being a self-published author. They are, in effect, your publisher, and you are paying them to be published. They have no need to market your book, because their business model is based not on your success, but on a steady stream of want-to-be authors lining up to pay for the same startup services.

To be a true self-publishing author, you have to, in effect, become your own publisher. You pay the costs, but you own the editing, the design, the printed books, and you keep the all publisher profits.

The print-on-demand aspect of these businesses, however, is not always bad. In some cases—depending on the company—it can be a good option for someone who doesn't need very many copies of their book and doesn't mind the high unit costs and lower print quality. Generally speaking, the traditional method of higher quality *process printing* is only economical if you need as many as 1,000–3,000 or more copies of your book (typically, a good self-promoting author can cover all his or her editing, design, prepress production, and printing costs once they sell 700–1,000 copies). If you only need 100 copies or fewer, however, then print-on-demand makes sense. And, if one does use a print-on-demand service, one can still improve other aspects of the book's quality, such as the editing and design. That is, even if you use print-on-demand, you can shop around independently to get the best editing, design, and prepress production that you can find.

> **Tip** The best practice for success is to hire the same professionals that publishers use for their most important projects.

WHEN TO USE PRINT-ON-DEMAND

The ideal way to use print on demand is for short-run printing, such as copies for advance publicity and market testing. It also is not bad if you plan to sell directly or to sell online. Have someone else do the editing, design, prepress work, and be sure to buy your own ISBN directly (explained in Chapter 3, *Getting Started*). That way, you are in control of your investment and in a better position to protect it. If you later decide to print more copies using the traditional process printing method, you will be able to do this without losing your original investment with the print-on-demand company.

> **Tip** Whatever the skills your project requires, today you can find the right people for every task by searching print or Internet trade magazines and resources used by industry professionals.

You can get a better deal as a self-publisher if you go directly to a print-on-demand provider that works with publishers, such as Lightning Source, which supplies printing for many of the other online print-on-demand companies.

Be aware that print on demand also has serious limitations with regard to book sizes and hardback editions. You'll need a knowledgeable designer to guide you if you want to use this option without needlessly increasing your production fees or limiting the aesthetic potential of your book. I'll provide a closer look at must-know printing issues in Chapter 8, *Your Publishing Options: eBooks, Print on Demand, and Process*

QUICK GUIDE | BOOK PROFESSIONALS

TASK	INDUSTRY PROFESSIONALS
1 Writing (organization, etc.)	➡ Developmental editor
2 Editing/proofreading	➡ Copy editor and proofreader.
3 Bookcover and page design	➡ Book designer
4 Prepress production	➡ Typesetter/page compositor, editor/proofreader
5 Printing the book	➡ Printing company (This may include paper suppliers as well as any service providers for things that must be outsourced, such as special binding, die cut tabs, etc.)
6 Marketing the book and marketing materials	➡ Publicist, graphic designer, and printing company
7 Distribution and fulfillment (storing and delivering the book to the marketplace)	➡ Distributors and Fulfillment services

Often, one editor can do all the different types of editing you require as well as the proofreading—but use an editor who has experience with books. Many graphic designers can do front covers, but not all will be able to do the cover production reliably. To ensure that the files work when delivered to the printer, the interior page design is best left to a designer skilled in book design. Many book designers can also do the typesetting and prepress production (i.e., page layout and digital file preparation.) In fact, a designer who understands all the design and production requirements for books is highly advantageous. For best results with printers, only use a printer with experience with books—preferably one that only or primarily does books.

Although many companies try to offer all or many of the above services, the best practice is to find the professional most skilled in the particular task, or tasks, without increasing your own project management requirements and time by working with too many different service providers.

Not included in the above list, but recommended, is an intellectual property rights attorney to help you review and/or craft your contract agreements.

Simplify the publishing process

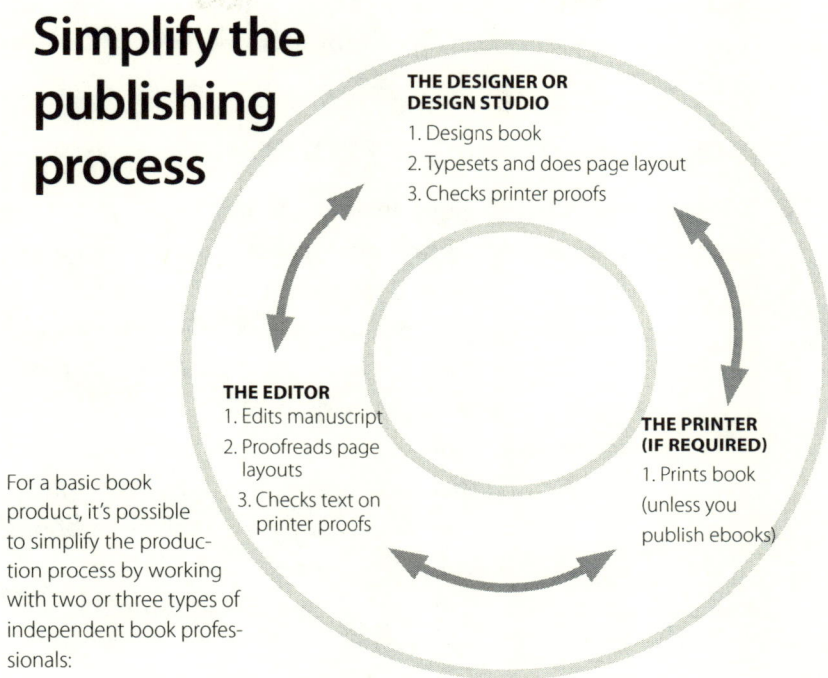

THE DESIGNER OR DESIGN STUDIO
1. Designs book
2. Typesets and does page layout
3. Checks printer proofs

THE EDITOR
1. Edits manuscript
2. Proofreads page layouts
3. Checks text on printer proofs

THE PRINTER (IF REQUIRED)
1. Prints book (unless you publish ebooks)

For a basic book product, it's possible to simplify the production process by working with two or three types of independent book professionals:

- **Editor/proofreader.** The person who can both edit your manuscript and proofread the page layouts and printer proofs.
- **Designer or design studio.** The person(s) who can design the book, typeset and layout the pages, and check the print quality. Designing the book includes creating and manipulating cover art and inside art, selecting fonts, determining the page layout specifications, deciding a color palette, etc.
- **Printer.** The company that will print the book. This assumes you're not publishing solely an e-book).

All three will know how to work with each other to complete your project. This three-person arrangement is common among small publishers because many editors are also good proofreaders, and many designers can also do typesetting, page layout, and check print samples. Locating one of the three may be all that is required to find the other two book professionals, because they are used to working together and have good contacts. It's not normally the case that editors or printers are good designers, or that designers are good copyeditors. Printers sometimes do have good typesetting and page layout services available. But be wary of any one person who says they can handle all three areas.

Printing. There I will also answer questions about converting print-on-demand book files into files for higher quality process printing.

IDENTIFYING THE RIGHT PROFESSIONALS

Getting a book done right involves understanding certain realities about the publishing industry. The quality of a book depends on good editing, good design, good production, and good printing. Some publishers use staff editors and designers, but, for their important projects, they tend to use freelance or independent expert workers.

Independent service providers tend to work harder and do superior work than their lower-paid on-staff counterparts. In order to ensure that your book is as good as the best books produced by the professional publishers, you need to work with the same independent book professionals that publishers use for their best projects.

To get expertise, talent, and experience, go to the independent professionals who make their living competing with each other every day for the best projects from the best publishing companies. It is this competitive marketplace that generates the most innovation and offers the highest quality work at the best price.

It's easy to identify the types of professionals you may need by looking at the simple Quick Guide to Book Professionals on page 28. This Quick Guide shows the main tasks involved in publishing a book and the kinds of professionals who can best help you at each stage of the project. Each stage in the publication of a book has its own level of complexity and its own professional requirements. A computer manual or cookbook, for example, requires more rigorous editorial/

proofreading review than a work of general fiction. Nevertheless, stated simply, there are seven main stages. These
stages, especially marketing, are sometimes interconnected
and overlapping with other stages.

Not every book has the same requirements, so your own
list of needed professionals may be much shorter or longer.
Some authors, such as those who, for example, are publishing
a book to be sold only from their own business location, may
require no publicist, no marketing materials, and no off-
sight storage or shipping. Other authors may have special
requirements that are in addition to the basic list (shown in
the Quick Guide: Book Professionals on page 28), such as
researchers, photographers, illustrators, cartographers, photo
retouchers, etc. They may also have collateral materials, such
as audio CDs that go with the book or require a custom
e-commerce Web site. Whatever the skills you require, go to
the trade magazines and Internet resources used by industry
professionals—resources such as the *Literary Market Place*,
Publishers Weekly, *How* magazine, etc. Visit bookstores and
look at books you like. Often the copyright page of a book
will list independent editors and designers involved in the
book's production.

Many professionals only advertise their services directly to
publishers through the Internet and/or direct mail campaigns,
but if you find professionals through the Internet, check them
out carefully. I once received an e-mail offering book design
services, but all their examples had been poached from one
unsuspecting designer in a different country. As it happened,
I recognized the designer's work and notified her. To make
sure the professionals you are hiring can deliver the quality
you want, always check their references, portfolio, and the

type of experience they have. Good professional editors, designers, and printers will all have happy clients willing to stand behind them.

Each of the seven stages of book publishing has its own requirements and challenges. In five of the following chapters, the first five tasks will be examined individually. The remaining two tasks—marketing and fulfillment—as well as advanced book design, will be explained in my book, *Book Marketing Essentials*.

When you get started in self-publishing, you will need to decide whether or not to create your own publishing company—a publisher name to go on your book in addition to the author name. A publisher name adds credibility to your product and increases your chances of success. In the next chapter, I will share some tips and resources for starting your own publishing company.

3

Getting Started

With true self-publishing, you are not merely an author, but a publisher as well. This being the case, you may decide you want to establish a publisher name to use with your book, especially if you plan to self-publish for profit.

You can establish a publishing company in a number of ways. You may, for example, want to simply publish the book under the name of your own existing business, or establish a new trade name or DBA ("doing business as") name for that purpose. If you don't already have a business, you will want to create one just for publishing purposes. I will not attempt to offer legal advice or detailed technical information about how to set up a new business or to do such things as determine your business structure or open a business bank account, and so on, because I am more narrowly concerned with the first five stages of self-publishing. I will, however, share some basic resources and information that may be helpful for authors who have never owned a business before.

If you are certain that setting up a publishing company isn't in your DNA, then you may want to skip this section. That said, I encourage you to look over this chapter anyway to better understand why it's both easy and beneficial. Creating a publishing company just for one book may seem over the top, but I'm not talking about an office tower filled with employees. Many small and successful publishers are really little more than one or two people with a vision, some business savvy, and contacts with talented independent service providers.

The key point is this—if you plan to sell your book, self-publishing the book under a publisher name will make marketing easier. This is true for two reasons. First, it will facilitate getting the retail resources you need to distribute your book more effectively and affordably (such as ISBNs and LCCNs— which will be explained later). Second, it will help your book look more credible, and there is no reason why your book shouldn't look as credible as possible when you are using professionals just like other publishers.

Tip Helpful information for small businesses is available online through the Small Business Administration's Web site: www.sba.gov/. This resource can help you with questions about the business structure best for you, legal requirements for business names, etc. To ensure compliance with any relevant federal, state, and local business laws, always seek advice from local authorities and professionals.

In addition to these perks, registering a business name can be advantageous when it comes time to pay taxes, and incorporation can limit some liability risks—which can be very important when it comes to some types of books. Also, if you decide to do additional books, then you're already set up for that, too.

SIX STEPS FOR GETTING STARTED

There are six basic steps to setting up your own publishing company:

1. Formulate a mission and brand identity.
2. Create and register a trade name.
3. Create and register an Internet domain name and set up an e-mail account.
4. Determine if you need a special physical mailing address.
5. Get a logo and business identity.
6. Get your publisher ISBN prefix, LCCNs, and barcodes.

1 **Formulate a mission and brand strategy:** If you are ambitious and enthusiastic enough about your book project to want to create a publishing company, then it is worth formulating a clear mission and brand strategy. Neither must be grand. These things are likely to evolve over time, but you can make a start by thinking through why your book exists, why people should care about it, for whom it is intended, etc., and what outward expression (brand identity) fits best with this understanding.

The mission you formulate can guide your selection of a publisher name, a Web domain name, the Web site design, the logo and trademark design, and all associated communications and visual appearances. Even if you start out with a simple plan written on the back of a coffee shop napkin, it can help you implement a consistent look and navigate many of the crucial decisions you'll make as you set up and evolve your company.

2 **Choose and register a trade name:** For license and tax purposes you will need to register your publishing business if you do not already have a business or institution that you can use for publishing purposes. There are different business structures you can choose, such as *sole proprietorship, limited liability company* (LLC), etc. A sole proprietorship is someone who owns an unincorporated business. This is the most common form of business structure and is simple to form and operate. The limited liability company structure is similar to a corporation. With this structure, you have limited personal liability for the debts and actions of your LLC. It offers greater legal and tax advantages, but is more complicated to set up.

You will likely find the process of setting up a small business much less intimidating if you join your local Chamber of Commerce. They usually have regular meetings, and you can make some friends and meet people who have already gone through the process. You might even sell some books!

You can often start a business in the state where you live using your own personal name and then later register a trade name—i.e., a separate name to do business under. You will need to register this trade name through your Secretary of State office in the state where you operate your business and, if desired, for wider marketplace protection, through the U.S. Patent and Trademark Office (USPTO). Both steps can now be done entirely online.

You are required to register your trade name in the state from which you intend to operate, but you do not have to trademark the trade name in order to use it for business purposes. That said, there are definite benefits if you do, such as creating a public notice of your claim of ownership of the trade-

Tip If you are unfamiliar with the legal and tax benefits of different business structures, consult a business attorney and/or certified public accountant.

mark and your exclusive right to use it in connection with the business description listed in the registration. Getting these matters straight from the start is important for many reasons, not the least of which is that you may be spending money printing lots of books with your trade name on them.

When selecting a trade name, you will need to first make sure that it is not misleading and does not infringe on the rights of anyone who is already using that name or a similar name. An intellectual property rights lawyer or professional with expertise in trademarks can be helpful. However, you may want to begin the selection process by conducting your own search through the USPTO Web site (www.uspto.gov/main/trademarks.htm). USPTO's online system allows you to search state and federal trademark registers to see if your proposed name is being used. You can also apply to register a trademark through the USPTO Web site for a fee.

In many ways, your brand identity and marketing begins with your selection of a trade name. So when you are thinking of possible names, think about how that name will be perceived by those people you want to buy your book. A good name is not always the most obvious one. It should be easy to say and remember, have positive associations, and be easy to defend legally. Also, think about how this name can be used in different methods of advertising and especially if it will be searchable on the Internet.

The nature of your book and business model will determine how important the Internet will be to you as a publisher. Some publishers don't need it at all. Others depend on it. If it is likely to be critical to your marketing and distribution plans, you may want to work on getting a domain name even before you select and finalize your trade name.

3 **Choose and register an Internet domain name:** When you choose a trade name, you may also want to acquire the same or a similar name for a Web address. Your Web address, or domain name, does not have to be the same as your business name, but if it is, it may make marketing easier. Unlike trade names, you do not register domain names through state or local governments; rather there are many online companies that will register it for you for a small fee. These companies will allow you to do free searches to determine if the name is already taken before you make a purchase. The important thing to know is that it is best to register sooner rather than later because of the growing competition for good domain names. You may also want to buy several similar domain names that can be pointed to one Web page address.

Tip Be sure to keep track of domain renewal dates. If you fail to renew on time, another business can acquire the name and attempt to sell it back to you at a higher fee.

When you register a domain name, it is for a specific duration of time, such as one to three years, and it must be renewed. Be sure to renew it on time or you may lose it.

You can have someone start designing your Web site before you get a domain name, but it is best to have the domain name before the design is converted into a working site. Once you have a site, or a placeholder page to announce the site, hire a hosting company to host your Web site. Some online domain name registrars also provide hosting services. That is, registering a domain and actually putting a Web site online are two distinct things.

Tip As soon as you have your domain name and Web site, you can start advertising your book. Don't wait until the book is printed to start your marketing campaign.

Most hosting companies also provide e-mail services, and with this service every e-mail you send contains your name and the actual domain address (i.e., your Web site address). This way, if you change hosting companies, you can keep and take your e-mail addresses with you. Open an e-mail account through the hosting company and have a Web designer simply create a simple temporary placeholder page with your e-mail link to take inquiries (such as one using "[your name] @" or "info@"). These addresses and your domain name can go on all your future advertising. You or your designer can upload the placeholder page to the site using a File Transfer Protocol (FTP) program. Have the designer build your Web site in a way that allows you to easily make changes to its content.

Programs used for building Blog sites and content management platforms, such as WordPress, Joomla, and Drupal may be good options. More about Internet advertising and e-commerce will be explained in *Book Marketing Essentials*.

4 **Determine if you need a special physical mailing address:** In addition to choosing a name that is also available as a domain name, consider whether you will use your home address or need to acquire a separate physical mailing address, such as a U.S. Post Office Box or a mailing service provided through businesses such as Mail Boxes Etc. and The UPS Store. This decision may depend on how likely it is for customers to unexpectedly drop in on you or how much mail your box needs to accommodate. If you anticipate a large volume of business mail and packages, then you will probably want to keep it separate from your personal mail. Remember, if you anticipate using Fedex or UPS, they do not deliver packages to PO Boxes.

5 **Get a logo and business stationery:** Registering and/or trademarking your trade name does not require that you create a logotype, or graphic brand icon, or symbol to go with it, but you may want to do so anyway. And, if you do have one created, you are not required to register it, but you can.

An icon and/or logotype are visual tools for branding your company and products. It represents your company identity. Used often and consistently, a well-conceived and nicely designed logo increases awareness of your business, inspires confidence in what your business does, and encourages customer purchases. It is a form of business equity.

For many companies, their logo becomes one of their main marketing tools and assets. A corporate logo is your highest-use graphic because it appears on everything your company does and produces. For this reason it's the most important single graphic a business will likely use and can often be the most expensive to acquire (regardless of complexity) from a production and legal point of view. That said, it's possible to start out small. If you only plan to publish one book, you are unlikely to have a reason to invest heavily in developing a company image.

A *trade name* is simply the name itself in whatever way it appears. A *logo* or *logotype* is the trade name written out in a specific font or custom letterforms. A *brand icon* or *symbol* is a graphic that goes with the trade name or logotype.

An effective business logo and/or icon will usually have certain qualities. It should, like the trade name itself, be distinctive and easy to defend legally. It should also be easy to recognize and work well in all the places it is likely to appear.

Here are a few simplified considerations for evaluating logotype and brand icons:

- **Functionality:** Is it easily identified and understood? Does it describe, convey, or express the central idea or mission of your publishing company? Will it stand out well in cluttered surroundings?
- **Versatility:** Can it be used in different media, sizes, colors, etc., without compromising its functionality? A logo should be easily recognized and work well in all the places it is likely to appear, such as your book's title page, the spine (a tall and narrow space), your company stationery, Web site, advertising mailers, etc. It can also be designed in a way that is adaptable to both single and multiple colors for different types of printing processes.

- **Defensibility:** Is it distinctive or too much like other logos in the same or different business categories? The more distinctive your logo, the more likely it can be defended in a courtroom. Avoid symbols such as depictions of books, which are overused in publishing. Defensibility is the reason that many modern corporate names express concepts and feelings, rather than business categories (such as Apple, Yahoo, Nike, etc.). Companies sometimes use a common name in combination with a symbol (McDonalds, Arbies, John Deere, etc.). You don't need to include words like "books" or "publishing" in your business name or use pictures of books or writing instruments for your symbol.
- **Retainability:** A good logo is memorable. This requires that it is distinctive, iconic, and not easily confused with other symbols, messages, or ideas.

How much or how little effort and cost you put into creating a company image is your decision and may depend on your budget and future publishing plans. You can start off with a just a trade name and no logo, or a simple black-and-white logotype. Or, you can have something designed more carefully in a way that is comprehensive and includes a detailed style manual that shows how to use the logo in different settings and publication methods. These issues are familiar territory to many experienced graphic designers. A designer can give you useful advice, concept the name and graphic, as well as create the final files or simply develop or clean up and render an idea that you provide.

If the graphic character of your logo is important to your business, you may want to take several trade name options to your graphic designer, because the designer may find that one option lends itself to development of a better graphic than the others. The name that sounds best may not be the name that looks best or works best for its intended uses.

Once you approve the final design, have the designer supply file formats suited for the different applications you need. Even if you plan to do business solely through the Internet, you will likely need to do some business transactions and marketing that will benefit from basic stationery, and especially business cards, with your logo, tagline, and contact information. It's useful to have your logo in different formats that can be used for all your likely print and Web applications.

Tip Before you purchase a font or stock photograph to use in a logo, check the license agreements. Some providers do not include commercial use or logo use under their general purchase fee. That is, you may have to negociate an additional usage fee.

6 **Getting publisher ISBN prefix, LCCNs, and barcodes:** As soon as you establish your publishing company, you will need to apply for a publisher's ISBN prefix. ISBN stands for "International Standard Book Number." It is a number that uniquely identifies books and book-like products. This number allows booksellers, wholesalers, and distributors to identify and order your books.

You can acquire this number from an ISBN Registration Agency. Bowker (R. R. Bowker LLC) is, for example, the exclusive ISBN Registration Agency for the United States.

More information about ISBNs is available online at: www.isbn.org/standards/home/index.asp. Self-publishers in the U.K. can find what they need at: www.nielsenbook.co.uk. For all other countries, visit www.isbn-international.org/en/agencies.html.

Once you have purchased a block of ISBNs for your publishing company (sold in a minimum block of 10 numbers at a time), you can use BowkerLink to add your book to your publication listing in Bowker's *Books In Print.* This resource is an essential bibliographic tool for libraries, booksellers, and publishers. For more about Bowker-Link, visit: www.bowkerlink.com/corrections/common/home.asp. Even if you have only one book, bear in mind that every new edition of your book requires a distinct ISBN.

Use your assigned ISBNs when purchasing barcodes for your books. You'll need barcodes with the proper ISBN to sell your titles through book retailers, wholesales, and distributors. You can acquire barcodes online at www.bowkerbarcode.com/barcode/.

You may also want a Library of Congress Card Number (LCCN). This number makes it easier for libraries and book dealers to access the book's bibliographic record and to better process orders. This is obtained by submitting an application over the Internet through the Library of Congress' Preassigned Control Number Program. More information about this is available online at http://pcn.loc.gov/. They will send you an e-mail with the number and the basic information about your book (title, author, place of publication, date, etc.) converted to a machine-readable cataloging record (MARC record) ready to be inserted on the back (verso) of the title page, preceded by the legend: Library of Congress Control Number.

QUICK GUIDE   HOW TO USE YOUR ISBN

- Any service provider (other than R. R. Bowker LLC) that supplies you with your ISBN will be registered as your publisher. That is, the number is registered to them through Bowker, rather than registered to you. This can never be changed. To avoid this, you must purchase from Bowker directly.

- Always print the ISBN with the letters "ISBN" included and each part separated by a hyphen. That is, for correct presentation, the digits of a book ISBN (ISBN-13) must be divided by hyphens into its five parts: XXX-X-XXXXX-XXX-X. The five sections are identifiers that represent 1) the prefix element mae available by EAN international, 2) a registration group element that identified the country, geographical region, or language area participating in the ISBN system; 3) the registration element that identifies the publisher, 4) the publication element that identifies the book title or edition; and 5) the check digit. For more about these categories and the mysterious check digit, visit www.isbn-international.org/en/manual.html.

- Print the ISBN on the verso (back) of the title page (copyright page) and at the bottom or foot of the outside back cover where it is visible if the book is wrapped in plastic. If the book has a jacket, print the ISBN on the bottom of the outside back jacket. It is not a bad idea to include the ISBN on the back of the case on case bound books.

- Include the complete ISBN in catalogs and all promotional materials. Your ISBN is how your book is identified, and it is only useful when all digits of the number are displayed.

- An ISBN can never be used for other products or variations of the same product. Once an ISBN is assigned, it cannot be reassigned. This is true even for book titles that go out of print. Your ISBN is a tool for identification and order fulfillment. The ISBN is a bibliographic element entered in national and international databases. It is printed on catalog cards and in catalogs.

- Regardless of price change, you must maintain the original ISBN on reprints of the same edition.

- You must use a separate ISBN for other editions, bindings, and formats in which your particular title is published, such as paperback, hardback, ebook, and also editions like audio books, microfilm, Braille. In addition to formats, any editions with significant changes to the contents require a different ISBN.

(continued on next page)

> | QUICK
> | GUIDE
>
> # HOW TO USE YOUR ISBN *(continued)*
>
> - One ISBN must be assigned to the complete set of volumes if a title is to be sold as a multi-volume set. Individual volumes being sold separately must each be assigned an individual ISBN. Both ISBNs—the ISBN for the individual volume and the ISBN for the set need to be printed in each volume, like this:
>
>   ISBN XXX-X-XXXXX-XXX-6 (Volume 1)
>
>   ISBN XXX-X-XXXXX-XXX-8 (5-Volume Set)
>
> - Any books kept in print over a long period of time (i.e., your backlist) should be numbered and published in your publisher catalog.

Once you've completed the 6 steps listed above, you will be well on your way to having a publishing company of your own that will help you produce and market your book more effectively. By having your own publishing company—a clear company mission, company name, Internet presence, mailing address, logo, and publisher's prefix (ISBN)—you will increase the likelihood of marketing, distributing, and selling your book successfully. Completing these steps will be especially helpful if your book is a business success and you wish to carry on introducing additional books and related products.

Self-publishing can be much more than simply writing a book and getting stacks of printed copies that nobody really wants. Done right, self-publishing is about letting people know that your book exists. It's about creating perceptions

▶ **STARTING A PUBLISHING BUSINESS**

The Small Business Administration's Web site is at: www.sba.gov

To find your Secretary of State Office online for registering your business, changing a business status, or adding a trade name, go to: www.statelocalgov.net/50states-secretary-state.cfm
Select the state and look for links to features such as "start a business" and/or "doing business as."

▶ **TRADE NAME SEARCHES AND REGISTRATION**

The U.S. Patent and Trademark Office (USPTO) is available at: www.uspto.gov/main/trademarks.htm
Their online system allows you to search all state and federal trademark registers to see if your proposed name is being used. You can also apply to register a trademark through the USPTO Web site for a fee.

▶ **PUBLISHER'S ISBN PREFIX, LCCNS, AND BARCODES**

ISBN Registration Agency. In the United States go to: www.bowker.com/products/isbnagency.htm
In the United Kingdom go to: www.nielsenbook.co.uk
More information about ISBNs is available at: www.isbn.org/standards/home/index.asp
Use BowkerLink to add your publication listing to Bowker's Books In Print and Ulrich's databases. For more about BowkerLink, visit: www.bowkerlink.com/corrections/common/home.asp
Acquire barcodes online at: www.bowkerbarcode.com/barcode
For Library of Congress Card Numbers (LCCN) visit: pcn.loc.gov/

about your book so that people will be interested in it. It's about creating a quality product that people will want. It's about customer relationships—the buyer's experience when they purchase the book and the reader's experience when they hold and read the book. All these things are influenced by how well you are set up to market and sell your book, and how well the book is written, edited, designed, and printed.

If you're like many writers, you want to get published as fast as you can. You never wanted to get into the business of publishing. But if you cannot sign with a publisher, you may have no choice but to self-publish. My advice is this—take your time and don't be discouraged if you don't like the business side of publishing. There are ways to get things done that can be very rewarding. Also, I will give you tips for how you can start off small, do things gradually, and limit your startup investment, without sacrificing the quality of your book project

4

Manuscript Preparation

The purpose of this chapter is not to tell you how to be a writer, but rather to help you put your manuscript into order so that when you, as the writer, hand your manuscript to an editor and designer, it is complete and ready for those services. This involves 1) steps for getting the book's basic concepts in good order and steps to make sure the book is complete, and 2) getting the physical (or digital) manuscript ready for editing.

There are nine important steps that many authors can follow during the writing process itself that will help put a manuscript into proper order, ensure that it is complete, keep it protected, and save you money by reducing the time required in editing and designing the book. Following some or all these steps will help you to expedite the workflow through the later stages of publishing as well. In fact, if many of these things are not done, it is likely that when the book comes back from the editor, designer, or typesetter you will discover problems that require so many changes that you may end up starting over. I will explain each of the following steps to help you reduce the chances of having to pay for the same services more than once.

1. Create your manuscript file using a word processing program.
2. Create a written book proposal.
3. Create a book "elements" checklist (see the Book Element Checklist on page 55).
4. Decide on a "house style."
5. Properly back up and label the digital manuscript file.
6. Save your research documentation.
7. Organize and prepare the book art for production (see the Book Art Checklist on page 63).
8. Prepare the manuscript for design.
9. Feed the spirit to stay motivated.

Here's a closer look at each of these steps:

1 **Create your manuscript file using a word processing program.** When you start work on your manuscript, type it using a word processing program. Most authors today are using Microsoft Word. Many computers come with free word processing programs, such as Apple's TextEdit, that are easy to use and more than adequate for the task.

If you're using an older computer, or old software, be sure you can export or save the files in a format that can be used by your editor.

2 **Create a written book proposal and book outline.** A book's appeal as a product often depends on its conceptual strength. Does it have a reason to exist and for whom? How is it unique? You can help yourself answer these questions and pull your book into shape by first writing a book proposal. Book proposals can include many things, such as a cover letter, sample chapters, and other features authors use to secure an agent or publisher. Be concerned most with three things that are part of any good proposal and useful even to self-publishing authors:

- Determine the book's topic category or categories.
- Determine the book's unique selling proposition.
- Have a marketing and branding proposal.
- Have an outline of the entire book and/or a chapter-by-chapter synopsis.

The main part of your book proposal only needs to be a page in length. Write your proposal before you write or finish the book and update it as needed. An early proposal will be useful for formulating a marketing plan and for helping you, the author, see how the manuscript is developing and whether it is staying on track or not. The proposal can be used as a source of information for the design brief. That is, it can be given to the designer to help provide art direction.

To create the proposal, start by identifying the book's category. The most general categories are trade books, professional books, scholarly books, etc. Each of these categories has subcategories. Trade books, that is books sold through bookstores, include fiction, such as romantic novels, science fiction, fantasy, poetry, short stories, etc., and non-fiction, such as self-help books, how-to books, biographies, auto-biographies, etc. Identifying a category for your book is a way to clarify both the book's conceptual requirements and the likely readership for your marketing efforts.

Once you have the right category for your book, write at least a short marketing and branding proposal—meaning, who will be the likely readers, and how you plan to reach and connect with them. Think of how you want your book to be perceived and include a short description. This marketing proposal is for your own private consideration. You don't want to give away all your ideas to everyone you'll be working with, but you can use this for formulating editorial and design briefs that can play a useful part in your overall planning, from how to write your book, to how you want it edited and designed. For more about marketing and branding your book product, see *Book Marketing Essentials*.

Identify the book's unique selling proposition, as this is one way of determining whether the book's idea is worth pursuing, what parts of the book are more important than other parts of the book, and what should be stressed when marketing the book. That is, determine why this book needs to exist and how it is unique from other books competing against it in the same category. Always keep the unique selling proposition in the forefront of the book's planning and development.

Next, write an outline of the whole book. This is not the same as a table of contents. In a table of contents, you can list chapter titles, which may or may not convey what the book is about. An outline is different in that it lists and conveys the actual ideas, concepts, and topics covered in the book. Ask yourself if each part of the outline fits together, is the sequence logical, is it complete? If the outline makes sense and conveys a complete picture of the book, then you're ready for the next step.

3 **Create a book "elements" checklist** (see the Book Element Checklist on page 55). Book elements are those things that make up the book and which are distinct in style from one another, such as heads, chapter titles, pull quotes, boxed explanations, etc.

When my company, RD Studio, started accepting book projects from self-publishing authors (as opposed to only from publishing houses), one of the first things we noticed was that some of the manuscripts were not complete, even though the authors believed that they were ready to go to press. The manuscripts had, for example, no front matter or end matter, or no table of contents or chapter titles. The reason for these omissions wasn't because the author intended it that way—they simply didn't know that they needed to do this work themselves, or they had simply neglected to think about many of these things. Whenever these omissions were pointed out, the authors would, of course, want to fix them. This meant the project would be put on hold while the author carried on with the writing. In such obvious cases, we noticed that the manuscript was incomplete, and we could let the author know before any work was done so no needless re-design or new page layouts were required.

If you don't put these things in order, don't expect designers or printers to spot the problems. Designers and printers are not editors and do not consider it polite or appropriate to critique client work. In fact, you can't count on companies caring to point out such omissions even if they spot them. After all, the more you have to correct your book and issue new editions, the more profit your providers stand to gain. You can help yourself avoid such costly mistakes by going into the process armed with a book elements checklist.

Different types of books contain different elements. Some books require very few elements while others require many. A book may have a certain amount of boxed information or sidebars for each chapter. A book may have an index, and, in fact, some may have several, one index for subjects and another for surnames. But whatever type of book you have, write out an elements checklist and make sure you have all the elements that belong in the manuscript.

Tip A well-written manuscript saves editorial and design time and that saves money.

See the the Book Element Checklist shown opposite for some typical book elements.

It is possible for the editor or designers to identify and add some of these features if they are missing from the manuscript pages, such as the half-title page, title page, and even a table of contents. However, it is always better if all intended elements are created and included by the author, especially the table of contents, as this is another tool that will help the author see whether the manuscript is complete and will ensure better accuracy. The publication data can be added to the copyright page after the book is typeset, but getting a copyright page laid out in order early on can prevent later delays. With regard to the index, this should be created only after the manuscript is typeset and proofread at least once so that page numbers won't be changing and can be added at the same time that the index is created.

It is also possible for editors and designers to interpret simple manuscripts and understand the difference between chapter titles and A-headings (A-head). Such manuscripts

BOOK ELEMENT CHECKLIST

Books vary greatly in contents, but you can use the list below as a checklist for identifying many of the typical elements found in books that must be prepared before the project is complete.

► *Front matter*

- ☐ Half-title page
- ☐ Title page
- ☐ Copyright page (most details, like publication data, credits, and disclaimers, can be placed later)
- ☐ Dedication
- ☐ Table of contents
- ☐ Foreword
- ☐ Preface
- ☐ Acknowledgments
- ☐ Introduction

► *The chapters*

- ☐ Chapter titles, and possible sub-titles
- ☐ Head levels (A-heads, B-heads, etc.)
- ☐ Special information elements, such as sidebars, pull quotes, boxed information, etc.
- ☐ Footnotes and/or endnotes

► *Art (photographs, illustrations, charts, figures, maps)*

- ☐ Labels
- ☐ Captions
- ☐ Sources and/or credit lines (including all URLs for Web resources cited)

► *Endmatter*

- ☐ Appendixes
- ☐ Notes
- ☐ Glossary
- ☐ Bibliographies
- ☐ List of contributors
- ☐ Index (not needed until the book is typeset and proofread)

require very little preparation. In other instances, more complicated manuscripts should have the elements marked up or coded so that they can be identified and designed consistently.

Book elements that are not altogether obvious to editors and designers, such as the material you want to have isolated into boxes or sidebars, or the different levels among the headings, should always be identified by you in the manuscript in some way. Usually, editors and experienced authors will "tag" the texts with codes, such as <box> at the beginning and </> at the end of text intended to go into a special box. This will be discussed in more detail on pages 67–71. If this seems like too much work, you can pay the editor to do it for you. A good editor can identify and properly tag the book's main elements as well as any material that can be placed into special elements such as sidebars before the book is sent to the designer.

4 **Have a "house style."** Making sure the spelling and punctuation is consistent with an established style is something that can be done for you by a professional editor. A good editor will always check for style inconsistencies, but the more you can do yourself, the less the editor will need to do. This saves both time and money.

What sort of inconsistencies should you be concerned with? Some authors learn how to spell certain words from the books they read. Likewise they pick up some punctuation styles from different books, unaware that books published in America use different conventions than those published in the United Kingdom and the rest of the world. In fact, in addition to the different conventions used by American versus British publishers, the different publishers within each country often have their own styles, sometimes called "house styles." These are extra style conventions to be used in the books they publish, whether academic, medical, business, etc. Style guides include such things as distinctive spellings of words, methods of abbreviation, capitalization and punctuation conventions, and how to list citations.

Tip Understanding and using a style guide in the early preparation of your manuscript can reduce the amount of editorial time and costs required to complete your publishing project.

The purpose of using a style guide is to ensure that the style is consistent throughout the manuscript and appropriate to the intended readers. Style inconsistencies can detract from an author's argument, confuse the reader, and become the target of criticism and bad reviews. Style consistency is especially important to the credibility of scholarly and academic publications.

It is not necessary to invent your own house style, rather you can choose from an existing style guide. Authors in America can, for example, use the very popular *The Chicago Manual of Style* for most publications. This substantive book includes most of the secrets of the book universe, such as many of the ins-and-outs of copyright law, author/editor responsibilities, as well as the expected pointers on punctuation and grammar. It also contains a catalog of fine details such as how to apply quotation marks to dialogues, when to write out numbers and when to use numerals, how to correctly abbreviate all manner of things, how to list entries in bibliographies including Internet citations, etc. Authors in the United Kingdom will find equivalent British conventions in *The Oxford Guide to Style* or *The Oxford Dictionary for Writers and Editors.*

Another popular choice is *The MLA Style Manual* published for the Modern Language Association. There are quite a few style guides available today.

5 **Protect the manuscript.** An author can help protect his or her manuscript by taking precautions to preserve the actual digital files and the ideas contained in those files.

Today, most manuscripts are typed in word processing programs. Authors may type all the manuscript into one file or try to minimize losses by putting each chapter into its own file. Either way, such processes are vulnerable to certain types of losses.

- Files can get corrupted, causing data loss.
- Files can get lost by mistaken file substitution and over-writing (such as over-writing completed earlier chapters with mislabeled later chapters).
- Files can get mislabeled and lost or deleted by mistake.
- Files can be created in programs incompatible with the programs used by the professionals you will want to hire.

The key to successfully protecting your data is making multiple and progressive copies or backups, using labeling conventions less prone to errors, and saving copies on different media other than your main computer's hard drive.

Proper labeling and filing of files will, for example, help ensure that you don't pay to have someone edit the wrong files, or end up sending the wrong (unedited file) to the designer and/or typesetter.

File labeling and progressive backups

The best way to avoid these losses is to make progressive editions and copies of a file, always saving some recent earlier files in case they are needed to recover data. You can work on a file for weeks, saving it every hour, but if it gets corrupted, you will have nothing unless you saved a version with a different file name at some earlier time before the corruption occurred. For example, while writing a chapter, save the file "chapter1-1." After each time you save the file, change the label to a higher edition number— "chapter1-2, chapter chapter1-3, and so on.

Be careful about putting files in folders labeled "final book" as it is likely that the book will be corrected and updated many times and you may, by mistake, pick up an earlier file from the folder labeled "final" rather than the most recent copy saved somewhere else on your hard drive. It is preferable to use folder labels such as "1st draft," 2nd draft," "1st edited manuscript," "1st printer copy," 1st revised printed copy," etc.

Tip Do not discard the electronic files just because the editor, designer, or printer has a copy. Always archive your own backups.

Archive your files

Back up files onto a separate computer hard drive, pen drive, or remote server and burn backup CDs with copies of files sent from editors, designers, and the printer. Do not discard the electronic files on your computer just because the editor, designer, or printer has a copy. Archive your own copy. Keep an archive of your last text files and the designer's files sent to the printer.

It is possible that if files get too old, no one will have a software program version that can open the files and recover the texts. Having an edited version of the plain text file may come in useful.

Because of software license agreements, designers cannot always legally send you an archival copy of the fonts used in the typesetting, but they can furnish a list of fonts and their sources. You do not need to purchase the fonts, but keep the list of those fonts on file in case it is needed in the future. And, as a final precaution, keep a physical copy of the printed book.

Non-disclosure agreements

In addition to digital file precautions, some authors may want to protect their work with non-disclosure agreements (NDAs). Non-disclosure agreements can be extremely long and detailed or short and concise. Each author needs to determine the degree of legal protection needed and who needs to sign it (editor, designer, printer, agent) before handling the manuscript. Such determinations may require hiring a legal professional.

6 **Save your research documentation.** Some authors gather information without documenting where it is coming from, and then when the manuscript is received by the editor or layout artist, it becomes apparent that all this data has to be recovered to check and finish the book—sometimes a difficult and time-consuming task that may not always be successful.

Authors who cite publications can prevent much needless loss of time by keeping scans or photocopies of the original sources for quoted material, plus copies of the copyright page of the publication. The best practice is to keep everything that is needed on file with the manuscript so that the editor can check your typed version with the original sources to ensure accuracy and to resolve any confusion over possible type errors in the quotes. If a bibliography is added to your book later, you will have these resources to create it

> **Tip** Be sure you save all the documentation necessary to prove you have obtained all necessary permissions and/or own the copyrights or other rights to all the material you publish.

and you will also be able to credit your sources correctly. Keeping a copy of the original copyright page and citation page number will usually provide sufficient documentation for credits and bibliographies.

When collecting art for a project, whether photographs or illustrations, create a file for any information that will be necessary to create captions, labels, or credits to go with the art. In addition to documenting your sources, you may need to get written permission for some citations. These permissions should be sought as soon as possible to avoid later delays, and a permanent record of each permission should be kept in a safe place.

7 **Organize and prepare the book art for production.** That is, put together any art files, such as photographs or illustrations for your manuscript (see the check list opposite).

Label your art files

Once you are sure that you have all the art files required, check to see if the files are labeled efficiently. For a book with a large quantity of art files, it is useful to label the art in a way that enables the files to be easily identified by chapter and order and/or type. A photo might be labeled "Photo2-1" (meaning chapter 2, photo 1 in that chapter) to distinguish it from other art-like illustrations (Illo2-1), figures (fig2-1), and tables (table2-1). Mark where the art placement should occur in the manuscript with a simple notation like: <photo1-1>.

It is also useful to have a printout of each piece of art with the label and caption included on it. This printout can be inserted into the printout of the manuscript. This way the editor can see the art and check the caption when working on the manuscript and the typesetter and designer can identify the correct art and its intended placement without having to open and examine each digital file.

Don't send original art

For books that require art—photographs, illustrations, charts, diagrams, etc.—it is useful to convert all the required

---

✓ BOOK ART CHECKLIST

All illustrations and photography has similar digital preparation standards and legal concerns. You can save time and money be being sure it is organized, labeled, and prepared correctly.

- ☐ Is the art complete? That is, does the art package contain all the image files required.
- ☐ Are the art files labeled efficiently?
- ☐ Is all the art digitized at the right resolution? (Resolution issues are explained in this chapter.)
- ☐ Do you have backups?
- ☐ Do you have any needed captions and or credits lines?
- ☐ Do you have a license or usage agreement?

---

art into a digital format and file the originals in a safe place. Avoid sending original art to agents, editors, designers, or printers. It is sometimes necessary to send the art to a service that will scan it or to a photographer who can photograph it. Only use sources whom you can trust, ideally those who have a reliable reputation or who will allow you to be present with the art. Insurance is small consolation when irreplaceable originals are lost or destroyed and the work must be deleted or recreated.

Get the art digitized at the required resolution

When the art is digitized, be sure that the color scans or photographs are 300 ppi (pixels per inch) resolution or higher for the actual size that will be used in the printed book. Otherwise, if process printing is used, the images will appear blurry. If a book is going to be 6" × 9", for example, and you want the art to fill the full page, then no dimension of the digital files can be less than 6.25" width and 9.25" tall when set to 300 ppi. The extra 0.25" is for each side (0.125 + 0.125 = 0.25)—that is, the extra image area that will be trimmed off at the edge of the page (called the bleed). Some printers require larger bleeds, though rarely more than .25" on each side. For black-and-white line art images, it is preferable to use higher-resolution files (1200–2400 ppi). The eye can detect a much larger range of grey tones than color tones, so ideally grayscale images should be much higher in resolution.

Skilled designers and layout artists can convert files to the correct format and even manipulate poor quality photographs so that they can be used to actually enhance the final publication. They cannot, however, convert low-resolution files into quality press-ready high-resolution files. Files prepared for the Web are only 72 ppi resolution, and unless they have large dimensions, they rarely have enough resolution to use in process printing. If they exist, you will need to find the original higher-resolution files. A 6" × 9" image for the Web converts to a print image roughly the size of a postage stamp (1.4" × 2.1"). Also, if you have a lot of large image files to upload to a designer, convert them to the RGB color mode if they are CMYK, and save them as JPEG files, rather than as TIFFs. This can reduce the file size by a fourth or more. Let the designer know that you have done that, and they can convert them to CMYK TIFFs.

Once the art is digitized to the correct size, follow the same backup procedures described above under the heading "Protect the manuscript."

Keep art labels and credits

Check to be sure you have all the captions for the art, any name labels that will appear in the book, and all the artist credit lines to be included as described above under the heading "Save your documentation."

Never use art without a license agreement

It is important to never use art if you do not have a license or usage agreement that allows you to use it for your intended purpose. Art—meaning any image, photograph, drawing, etc.—is protected under copyright law, and when you publish it you are creating tangible documentation for anyone's rights you may have offended. Copyright laws include such things as private buildings, people, and products that appear in images you use. That is, people and companies can own the image of their buildings and property. Be aware that photos of objects or art that are too old to be copyright-protected may also be protected—that is, the photograph itself may be copyrighted property.

Even if an artist "gives" you art, this may not entitle you to use it in a book. Some artists/photographers expect royalties if their art is used in a publication. In many cases it is worthwhile to pay royalties to get useful art. In other cases, it is possible to buy adequate royalty-free stock photography and/or illustrations for your project. Images sold with

> **Tip** Never use art if you do not have a license or usage agreement that permits you to use it for your intended purpose.

a "royalty-free" agreement do not always entitle you to use the art in the way or context you want, so be sure to read the license agreement carefully. Also, be aware that even when a stock image provider is selling an image with a license agreement, the image may not include model or property releases. That is, in order for an image to be used for commercial, funding-raising, or promotional purposes, permission in the form of a release must be obtained for any recognizable persons or private property in the image. Some images involve greater risks than others.

8 Prepare the manuscript. Even before you have completed the writing of your manuscript and have all the documentation ready to go to editing, it is useful to start "prepping" the file or files. This helps the work flow, especially when the manuscript goes to the editor and designer. Preparing the manuscript consists of basic page setup and keystroke steps that are easy to implement and an optional additional method involving design tags to identify the different elements you would like in your book.

Simple steps for easy manuscript preparation

You'll save time and get the best results if you follow these guidelines when preparing your manuscript:

- Place all the text—including extracts, tips, and text intended for special features such as sidebars—in one vertical double spaced column (the most common setup for a Word processing file).
- Make margins one inch on all sides.
- Turn off right, or full, justification so that all text is

left-justified only. This will preserve the correct word spacing.

- Turn off hyphenation. The only hyphens that should appear in the text should be hard hyphens (those keyed-in).
- Make paragraph indents with the tab key rather than the space bar.
- Use only one font. Avoid using sans serif fonts because the number 1 is hard to distinguish from the letter l and capital I. In other words, use a serif font, which has the extra marks on each letter (like this font used in this book), not like this font: sample sans serif font.
- Avoid using ALL CAPS for chapter titles and heads, or to distinguish any other elements. It is preferable that no text be typed in ALL CAPS. It often ends up slowing the workflow by requiring texts to be altered to fit the approved design.
- If you place art into a word processing text file, include a folder containing separate high-resolution files for all the art including your logo graphic. Include an art file label in the text file. Make sure the label in the text file matches the label on the digital file.

Design tags for book elements

In the same way an outline helps an author know if a book is complete and in logical order, it is useful for some books to have a list of special elements. For example, an author may want to have some explanations in the book boxed to make the book easier to use and more visually interesting. If so, the author will need to identify them so that the editor and designer know that they should be treated differently.

QUICK GUIDE	BOOK ELEMENT STYLE TAGS

Element style tags can be created for any new element used in a manuscript. If you're interested in this method, these are some typical style tags used by editors:

Chapter title	<CT>
Subtitle	<ST>
A-head	<1H> or <AH> etc.
B-head	<2H>
C-head	<3H>
Extract	<EXT>
Extract attribution or source	<ATTR>
Caption	<CAP>
Boxed text	<BOX>
Boxed head	<BOXH>
Sidebar	<SB>
Sidebar head	<SBH>
Sidebar Text	<SBTX>
Pull quote	<PQ>
Bullet list	<BL>
Numbered list	<NL>
Unnumbered list	<UNL>
Case study	<CS>
Tip	<TIP>
Text that must start on a new page	<page break>
Space between paragraphs	<line break>
Caps	<CAPS>

Additional instructions, like "set math symbol" or "set fraction" or "place art" can be placed in lesser/greater symbols <> to alert the designer.

If one chapter has material that benefits from special design treatment, the author may want to improve the usefulness of the book by including similar material in other chapters, too. Special elements may include such things as case studies, testimonials, different opinions, warnings, and tips. The author should not attempt to design these elements, rather the text for each element can be tagged so the designer can find it and create a suitable design for it. For example, if you have text you want in a box, tag it with the code <box> where it starts and tag it <end box> or </> where it ends. See the Quick Guide: Book Element Style Tags on page 68 for more tags you can use.

The best way to prepare a file is to do as little formatting or design as possible while you are writing it (use tags instead). That is, don't bother formatting or designing different elements of the manuscript yourself in the word processing file that will be delivered to the editor and later to the designer. Your design attempts will not be useful.

Formatting that can be done in word processing programs, such as boxed text, takes too much time and will not import properly into the page layout programs used by professional designers. Such formatting often gets either deleted or garbled and then the text has to be extracted meticulously and reformatted. Authors who attempt to format their book in word processing programs are wasting their time when they could be concentrating on writing and completing their manuscripts. Save yourself needless trouble and only use minimal formatting, such as italics and bold.

The best way for an author to indicate any desired formatting that is not self-evident (such as for chapter titles and main headings) is by using what are typically known as "style tags" or "tags." These tags are very simple letter codes that identify the different elements in the book.

It is useful for authors to do minor formatting, such as using bold and italics in the text or possibly making chapter titles larger and centered, but any special types of formatting should be indicated by tags. Even elements such as bullet lists and numbered list can be manually tagged, rather than using the automated word processing commands which may not import properly into some page layout programs. If you can't be bothered to tag, you can usually pay an editor to prepare and tag a manuscript for you.

Tags are the easiest method for the author, too. Tags require no author knowledge of the special styling commands available in word processing programs and no effort to try to keep things consistently aligned and "designed" as the author develops the text. That is, you, the author, do not need to spend time styling the text in any significant manner by using boxes or different fonts, etc., rather you can just tag the different elements and move on with your writing.

Unlike many of the "styles" in word processing programs, tags will always import, making designing and typesetting the book easier for the designer. Sidebars, for example, can be tagged quickly with a simple tag such as <SB>. The sidebar text has the tag <SB> at the beginning and </SB> or just </> at the end (i.e., a backslash for the end tag). When the designer sees the tags, he or she knows that the text between the tags is to be designed as a sidebar.

Each important or unclear element in the manuscript can have its own tag. Level-one subheads or A-heads, for example, can be tagged <1H> and level-two heads <2H>. This way there is no guessing whether a lone sentence in bold is an A-head or B-head or simply a sentence with emphasis. Sometimes it's sufficient to simply put a tag at the beginning of the element. Tags provide on-the-spot simple and exact instructions for the designer and typesetter that require no further interpretation to guess an editor's or author's formatting intentions.

Tags are not necessary when the book elements are self-evident. If a book has only A-heads, there is no need to mark them as A-heads because there are no other head levels to cause confusion. A simple manuscript that contains nothing more than chapter titles, basic text, A-heads, and a few extracts, doesn't require any tags.

Tags can be handwritten on a printout of the manuscript and this can be shipped along with the digital text files to the designer. If you do want to key-in the tags into the actual digital file (word processing program file), then the tagged file can be e-mailed and no marked hardcopy needs to be shipped. This saves time and postage.

The page layout person simply removes the tags when typesetting the book. Any special instructions for the designer and typesetter can also be put between the same lesser/greater signs <> and they will be removed later in the page composition stage.

Design should be left to an experienced book designer. Identify the elements of your book with simple tags and let the book designer provide you with design options. Once you approve the designs for each element, they can be implemented throughout the book consistently during the typesetting and page layout process.

9 **Feed the spirit.** Publishing a book can be very rewarding financially, and it can open up new and interesting opportunities in your life. Writing a book, however, can be hard work and some of the tasks can be tedious and even boring. For these reasons, some authors give up without ever finishing their projects. With that in mind, here are some suggestions for keeping your creative spirit alive:

- Do presentations and workshops: This is good beta testing for authors. Many successful authors find it easier to generate the content they need and improve its organization when they get out and give presentations and workshops. It enables them to see what does and doesn't work, and also how to say things better.
- Read about the topic you are writing about—especially those authors who are most current and respected in the field.
- Attend discussion groups and seminars on the topic you are writing about.
- Join up with would-be and professional writers for encouragement.
- If you can't find encouragement, at least tune-out the doubters, naysayers, and all sources of information you find discouraging.
- If you are procrastinating, identify the conflict causing you to procrastinate so that you can overcome it.
- Find ways to eliminate the distractions in your life—toss the radio and disable the TV. Let the world take care of itself for a while.

- Identify what motivated you to write in the first place, and what conditions under which you were or are most productive.

GHOST WRITERS

Have an idea for a book, but can't get motivated enough to write about it? Or maybe you have written parts of a book, but can't get around to finishing it because you are too busy or simply lack the necessary writing skills. If so, you may want to consider hiring a ghost writer. A ghost writer is a writer who will write or complete a book for you, and you will officially be credited as the author. Ghost writers usually write for either a flat fee or a royalty. These writers are called ghost writers because they remain anonymous.

Some writers can write well about nearly anything if they have enough material to work, such as hours of recorded interviews. Other people have a book in them or an interesting story to tell, but no time to write. Some bestselling autobiographical books published under the names of movie and sports celebrities were written by ghost writers.

Ghost writers are sometimes acknowledged for their help. Acknowledgment usually is not given because they are hired for their writing skills and not for any special expertise they had in the field. In other cases, crediting a ghost writer may diminish sales. Because some ghost writers do expect to be credited in the foreword or under the author name, the form of acknowledgement to be given or not given should be negotiated in advance, along with other details such as schedule, terms of payment, etc.

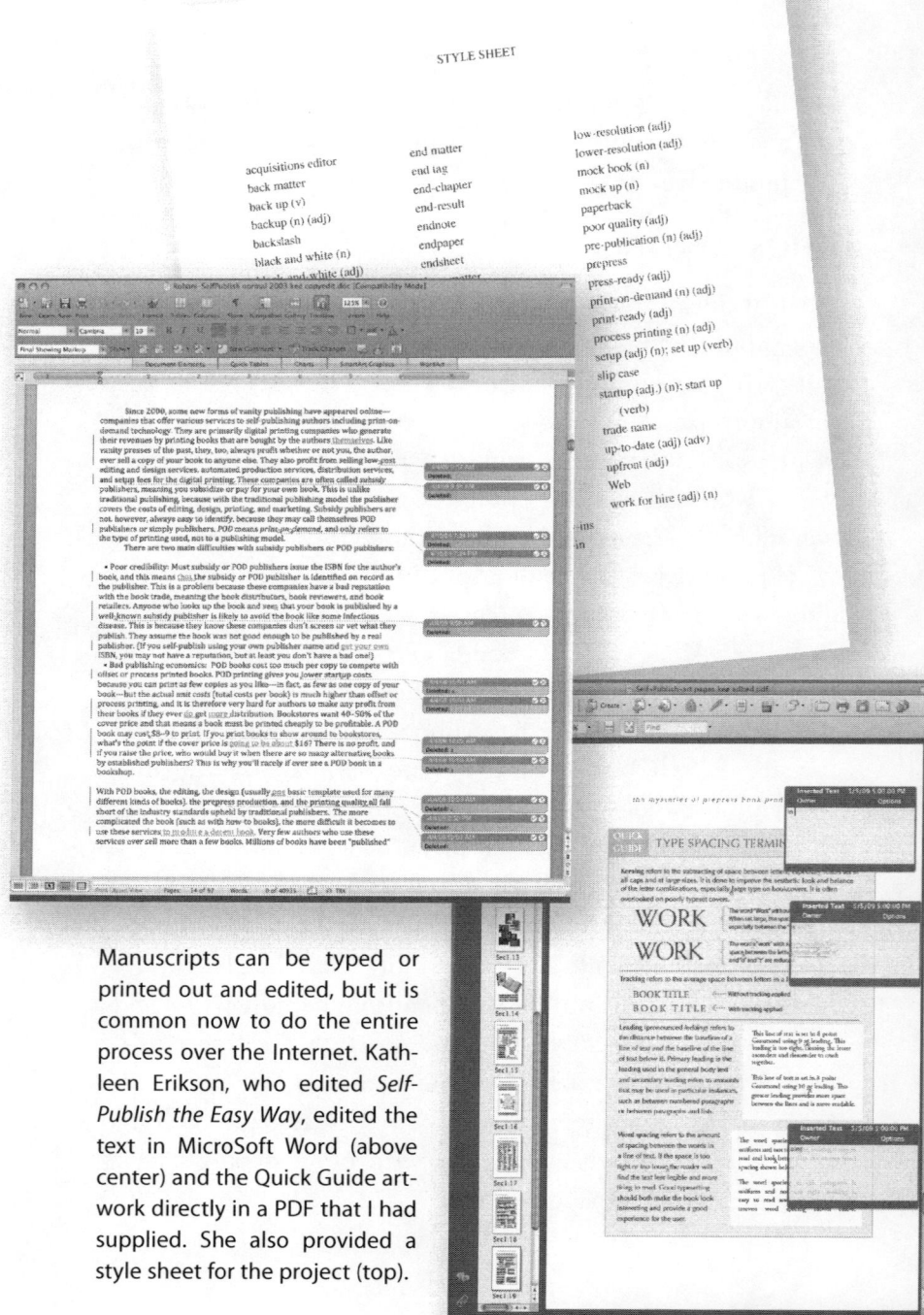

Manuscripts can be typed or printed out and edited, but it is common now to do the entire process over the Internet. Kathleen Erikson, who edited *Self-Publish the Easy Way*, edited the text in MicroSoft Word (above center) and the Quick Guide artwork directly in a PDF that I had supplied. She also provided a style sheet for the project (top).

5

Finding the
Right Editor

Hiring an editor may seem like giving in to an unwelcome and unnecessary assault on your god-inspired prose and an added and unnecessary pilfering of your bank account. But in reality, it is one of the best ways to safeguard your reputation and protect your publishing investment. It's well known that authors grumble about editors messing around with their writing, but in the end they are usually grateful for the help they receive, even if secretly.

An experienced author understands that the purpose of an editor is to discover mistakes an author is unlikely to see and to fix them so that the book is more useful and appealing to readers. Editing can involve reorganizing parts of the manuscript and working through hundreds of edits that correct errors and improve clarity. Submitting to this process requires humility and patience on the part of an author, but it has many worthwhile benefits.

Catching and correcting mistakes before typesetting and printing saves time and money. It can also save you from the embarrassment and consequences of unfavorable reviews. The typical first-time author who believes his or her book is too perfect to require any type of editing fails to understand the kinds of problems that are obvious to professionals, or, for that matter, obvious to many readers—such as chapter titles that don't match the table of contents or running heads. There may be critical omissions, needless repetitions, tangential information, misspelled names, confused sources, grammatical errors, and much more.

> Tip An editor is a good investment. Editors catch mistakes before they become costly to fix.

Very few authors will spot all the errors. But after the manuscript has been designed and typeset—that is, once it changes form—the author usually will see many problems that were overlooked. In some cases, an author may end up correcting the pages in an excessive number of back-and-forth proof rounds, spending as much or more money for keying-in new changes and repagination than would have been the case if he or she had hired an editor before the book was typeset.

When an author bypasses the editor and hands the book to a professional book designer, the book designer is not expected to proofread the manuscript for errors. If the problems don't impede the design, the designer is unlikely to notice them.

Designers read design briefs, not actual manuscripts. Moreover, professional book designers, typesetters, and layout artists usually don't feel it is their place to comment on content or about what they perceive to be possible editorial problems. They also will not act as proofreaders and neither will printers. A huge and embarrassing typo on the cover of a few thousand printed books is simply your problem. The printer will send page proofs to be checked before the book is printed, but it is up to the publisher—which means *you* if you are self-publishing—to check every word and line of text and any other matter on the pages before giving the printer the final okay to print. Any errors found after the books are printed are the legal and financial responsibility of the publisher (you), not the printer.

It takes a completely different set of eyes from the writer of the book to see all the problems. Even professional line editors discover more problems in a book they have already edited after it has been converted from manuscript to typeset pages. Minor grammatical or punctuation errors discovered after typesetting are normal and not a serious problem to fix, but any major rewriting should be sorted out before typesetting.

Tip Don't expect designers and printers to proofread your manuscript or to catch errors in it. As professionals, they don't judge or even comment on an author's writing. If you want an editor or proofreader, you need to hire one.

CHOOSING THE RIGHT KIND OF EDITOR

When looking for an editor, it is important to pick the right kind of editor for your needs and preferably one with experience in the same genre of books. There are two basic categories of editor that you need to know about: developmental editors and copy editors.

Developmental editors

To improve manuscripts and prevent problems caused by poor writing, publishers have *acquisitions editors* and *developmental editors*. An acquisitions editor, also known as a commissioning editor, will look over new manuscript submissions to determine if they fit the publisher's goals and marketing capabilities. If the manuscript passes this review, it will go to a developmental editor, or in some cases, the acquisitions editor will perform this function.

Developmental editors (also known as *structural* or *concept editors*) make sure the book is marketable and credible enough to withstand peer review. This involves looking at the purpose of the book and how the concepts are developed in the book, including the book's organization, completeness, and tone. The developmental editor will check to see if the ideas are presented in a clear and logical order, whether certain sections are unnecessary or incomplete, and so on. Far more serious than grammar or punctuation problems, some manuscripts have major concept problems that need to be fixed even before the smaller grammatical details are edited. Developmental editors are not concerned with *copyediting*, which involves finer details of clarity and flow such as grammar, punctuation, tense, and parallelism.

First-time authors with little writing experience usually require developmental editing. If you think your book is finished but you never wrote an outline or table of contents, you're probably in need of developmental editing. If you are

QUICK GUIDE DEVELOPMENTAL EDITORS

Developmental editors will typically provide a report that covers five main concerns and how they, can be improved. Most concerns can be expressed by a few basic questions:

► **CONTENT AND PURPOSE**

- Has the author achieved his or her goal, and if not, why?
- What is the intended and likely audience, and is the material prepared in a way that is suitable for that audience?
- Is any important content missing, and are there unnecessary and distracting matters that need to be eliminated?

► **ORGANIZATION**

- Does the content follow a logical order?
- Is the table of contents clear and sufficiently detailed?
- Does the book contain a sufficient narrative overview and transitions from one section to the next?
- Do the explanations and divisions provide easy document navigation?

► **DETAIL**

- Does the book have the appropriate amount of detail for the intended audience?
- Are maps, figures, and art suitable?
- Is the material sufficiently and appropriately referenced?
- Does the content convey problematic biases relating to race, religion, gender, disability, or any other legally protected status?

► **STYLE**

- Is the style, including vocabulary and grammar, appropriate for the intended audience?

► **TONE**

- Is the tone appropriate for the subject matter and audience?
- Is the tone consistent throughout?

an author who is fluent in your subject matter, conducts frequent seminars and workshops, and has experience writing, you are less likely to require major developmental editing.

If you feel you need a developmental editor, you should hire an editor who has experience with the type of book you are writing. If you are writing fiction, for example, you'll need a developmental editor who can check for character development and plot. A developmental editor can also give good insights into others matters such as pacing and mood. They also are ideal for authors who can gather all the facts needed for a book, but don't have the time or writing experience to put those facts into the clearest and most logical order. Different types of books require different types of editing.

Tip Sloppy editing or no editing may make you vulnerable to criticism from book reviewers.

Copy editors

Copy editors go through the book line by line, spotting errors, marking up corrections, and making recommendations to improve grammar and sentence clarity. This type of editing is sometimes referred to as *line editing*. Not every manuscript needs developmental editing, but even the most experienced authors usually benefit from some copyediting.

A major part of the work copy editors do also involves cross-checking. They will, for example, check the table of contents with the wording of the actual chapter titles on the chapters themselves, as well as any references to notes, tables, maps, and art, and point out any discrepancies. They

QUICK GUIDE	COPY EDITORS

There are many helpful things a good copy editor can do without attempting to rewrite your book or eliminate your voice by interfering with idiomatic expressions and unique figures of speech. Here is a list of some of the fixes you can expect from a copy editor:

► STYLE

The copy editor, in consultation with the author/publisher, will first determine a basic style approach for all mechanical edits (see below), usually based on an existing style guide such as *The Chicago Manual of Style*. The copy editor will also formulate styles for any special or unique categories not covered in a standard style guide, such as transliterations for foreign words or words to be italicized.

► CONSISTENCY (KNOWN AS *MECHANICAL* EDITS)

Copy editors will check the consistency of the text, such as abbreviation, capitalization, hyphenation, punctuation (use of ellipses, parentheses, quotation marks), and table and caption formatting. They will check for consistent usage of spelling conventions (such as American vs. British). They will also check the consistency of internal cross-references—meaning the consistency between references in the text to table and chapter figure numbers.

► SPELLING

In addition to looking for spelling conventions that are incorrect for the intended audience, copy editors will correct misspelled words.

► GRAMMAR

There are few hard-and-fast rules that everyone can agree on, but copy editors will examine sentences for issues such as verb tense and completeness. They will also make suggestions for eliminating ambiguities and unclear pronoun references, simplifying overly complex wording, putting sentence parts in a more logical order, and deleting unnecessary repetitions.

also will look for inconsistencies in how citations are made and look for any important omissions, such as permissions for art used.

In order to work with copy editors effectively, it is useful to understand the common proofreader or editorial marks used to indicate changes. Today, editors either work on a printout of the manuscript or in a digital file. In the early and primary editorial stage, the editor will work in the same word processing file used by the author or on a printout made from the author files. After a book is typeset, work is done on PDFs (portable document format). In the case of printouts and PDFs, many of the same markup conventions may be used before the project is completed. The traditional marks (shown in the Quick Guide: Proofreaders' Marks and Quick Guide: Proofreaders' Marks Applied on pages 84–85) are marks that you may also want to understand and use when communicating changes with your typesetter and designer.

In the first stage of editing, many editors will want to edit the files digitally, using the same word processing program that you used to write the manuscript. You will need to first save a copy of the original manuscript—a copy that should be labeled, dated, and never changed. This copy is used for reference purposes only. The editor will then return an edited copy that you can review. Using the editing features in the word processing program, you'll need to accept or reject each of the editorial suggestions. You may want to send the updated manuscript back to the editor to proofread your changes and so that they can see your comments on any major edits you didn't accept.

When you are satisfied with the editing, you can then send the manuscript to be typeset according to the design

FIND THE RIGHT EDITOR

Where to find an editor

These days it's fairly easy to find an editor online. You can, for example, go to the Editorial Freelancers Association Web site at www.the-efa.org and follow the link "find a freelancer" or the Bay Area Editors Forum Web site at www.editorsforum.org and follow the link "find the right editor". Although it is possible to simply search the Internet for editors, getting a professional referral is better. Other useful resources are the *Literary Market Place* and *Publishers Weekly*. The Editorial Freelancers Association has a link to a page (www.the-efa.org/res/rates.php) that provides common rates. Here are some other suggestions for how to select and work with an editor:

☐ Look for an editor with experience with books, rather than one who primarily does short college essays, advertising materials, or business résumés. Editors who are used to working on small projects may not have the experience or patience required for longer, more complicated manuscripts.

☐ Find an editor who can proofread typeset page layouts and check for typesetter errors. Often editors who work with publishers do proofreading, too, and this will reduce your project management requirements.

☐ Ideally, choose an editor who has experience in a similar genre of books. Editors with experience in certain types of books, such as business books, how-to books, or children's fiction, will have a better idea of the standards required and typical problems that occur with those categories of manuscripts.

☐ Ask for samples and referrals. Anyone can claim to be an editor.

☐ Have a contract that includes terms for schedule, anticipated costs, delivery method, copyright ownership of final edited work, any acknowledgement requirements, and a non-disclosure clause.

☐ Even if you hand over the whole manuscript, arrange to get a small sample edited before going further. Determine if the level of editing is helpful. Some editors will overreach while others will not do enough. A good author–editor relationship requires respect and good communication. It is part business and part chemistry. Make sure it is a good fit before you go too deep into the project.

QUICK GUIDE: PROOFREADERS' MARKS

If you are using printouts in the editorial stage, it is helpful to use accepted proofreaders' marks. These conventions can save time and reduce confusion. Margin marks are sometimes omitted or inserted in the text line.

Instructions to author and/or typesetter	Mark that appears in text	Mark that appears in margin
Delete	proofreaders' marks	ℛ
Delete and close up	proofreaders' marks	ℛ
Delete and leave space	proofreaders' marks	#
Leave as it was	proofreader's marks	stet
Insert new matter	proofreaders	marks L
Change to capitals	proofreaders' marks	caps
Change to small caps	proofreaders' marks	s.c.
Change to lowercase	Proofreaders' Marks	l.c.
Change to bold	proofreaders' marks	bold
Change to italic	proofreaders' marks	italic
Change to roman	proofreaders' marks	rom
Underline	proofreaders' marks	underline
Wrong font	proofreaders' marks	w.f.
Close up space	proofreaders' marks	⌒
Insert space	proofreaders marks	#
Reduce space	proofreaders marks	less #
Transpose	marks proofreaders	trs
Move to right	proofreaders' marks	⊏
Indent one em-space	proofreaders' marks	⊏m
Take over to next line	proofreaders marks	take over
Take back to prior line	proofreaders marks	take back
Spell out	8 oz of water	spell out
Begin new paragraph	proofreaders' marks	n.p.
Insert punctuation	proofreaders marks	⌄
Insert em-dash	proofreaders marks	m
Insert en-dash	proofreaders marks	n
Insert quotes	proofreaders' marks	⌄⌄
Insert parentheses	proofreaders' marks	{ }

PROOFREADERS' MARKS APPLIED

Editors and proofreaders tend to apply hard-copy proofreader marks with different degrees of legibility and in individualistic ways, sometimes omitting margin marks. The sample below is typical of what can be expected when an editor marks a printed manuscript. The example on the right shows the same text after corrections have been made by the typesetter.

Nowhere in Plato is there a deeper irony or a greater wealth of humor or imagery, or more dramatic power. Nor in any other of his writings is the attempt made to interweave life and speculation, or to connect politics and philosophy with. The republic is the center around which the other dialogues may be grouped; here philoso-phy reaches the highest point (especially in *Books V, VI, VII*) to which ancient thi... He was the gr... genius whom the... in hi... tha... thinker,... ...n... edge are co...

○/*run in*

¶

loose line

cap/#/rebreak

loose line

rom

Nowhere in Plato is there a deeper irony or a greater wealth of humor or imagery, or more dramatic power. Nor in any other of his writings is the attempt made to interweave life and speculation, or to connect politics with philosophy.

　　The Republic is the center around which the other Dialogues may be grouped; here philosophy reaches the highest point (especially in Books V, VI, VII) to which ancient thinkers ever attained. He was the greatest meta-physical genius whom the world has seen; and in him, more than in any other ancient thinker, the germs of future knowledge are contained.

specifications you have approved (that is, if the designer has already been working on the interior design while the editing was in progress). Once the edited manuscript is typeset, all future edits and proofreading will be on the newly designed page layout rather than in the word processing file used by the author and editor.

Designers usually don't use a word processing program to design books and will instead return the pages in a PDF or a printout created in a page layout program. Additional editing can be applied to PDFs or printouts and sent back and forth between the author, editor, and page layout artist. Many authors and publishers still use printouts, but today it is possible to complete a book without making any printouts for editorial and review purposes, which saves the expense of shipping marked-up manuscripts.

Proofreading is separate from editing, though some editors will do the proofreading for you, too. Proofreading has three stages. The first stage is when you are working with the editor on your manuscript. The second stage is when the manuscript is typeset and the page layouts are completed (discussed in Chapter 7, *The Mysteries of Prepress Book Production Explained*). The third stage involves checking the print proofs, i.e., samples of the actual book cover and pages provided by the printer (discussed in Chapter 8, *Your Publishing Options: eBooks, Print on Demand, and Process Printing*).

HAVE REALISTIC EXPECTATIONS

There are many editors willing to work directly with authors for very reasonable fees. That said, a good, reliable editor can sometimes be hard to find. When you do find one, you'll have a better chance of keeping the relationship if you have realistic expectations about what an editor does and how long editing takes.

First-time authors are often unaware of what is involved in editing and how much it can improve their manuscript. Those who submit to the process can be shocked when they see the number of suggested editorial corrections marked on the returned manuscript. They are likewise disappointed that, after having finished writing the manuscript to their own satisfaction, they need to read and correct it each time it comes back from an editor. Typically, an author can expect to read the manuscript after the first draft, or during however many drafts he or she creates, then after it has been edited, and then again after it has been typeset. At each stage, they will likely have their own changes that they will want to make, and each time alterations are keyed-in, the changes need to be checked or proofread to ensure that they went in as intended and didn't create any new problems of clarity or incorrect grammar.

Some authors are so experienced and so capable at writing that they require very little editing. In such cases, editing is little more than correcting minor details of punctuation and grammar. Over the years at RD Studio, I have seen hundreds of edited manuscripts from publishers, so I am not surprised to see pages covered in red editorial marks—usually on nearly every page. In fact, edited manuscripts are usually covered in marks. Once these changes are keyed-in and the book is typeset, it is not uncommon for the typeset pages to also end up with some more editorial marks that have to be keyed-in.

Well-written manuscripts typically go through a copyedit, where perhaps hundreds or even thousands of small changes and/or suggestions are made, and then through three "passes,"

The Editing Process

The diagram below provides a view of the basic stages of editing and proofreading in relation to the design process and prepress production (typesetting and page layout), leading into marketing and printing. These stages typically unfold in a coordinated and concurrent way that takes place over a period of a few weeks or months.

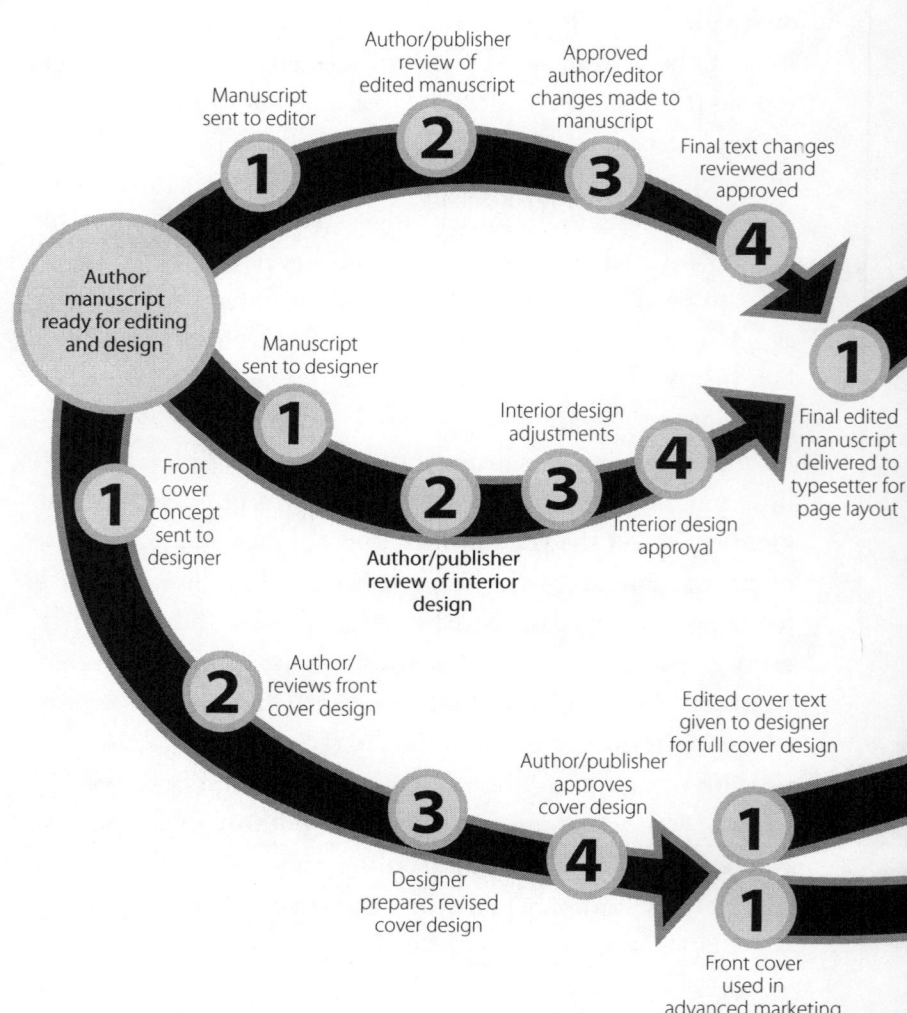

Professional publishing is rarely more efficient than shown below. Typically, a manuscript will go back and forth between an author and editor more than a few times, as will design revisions and typeset pages.

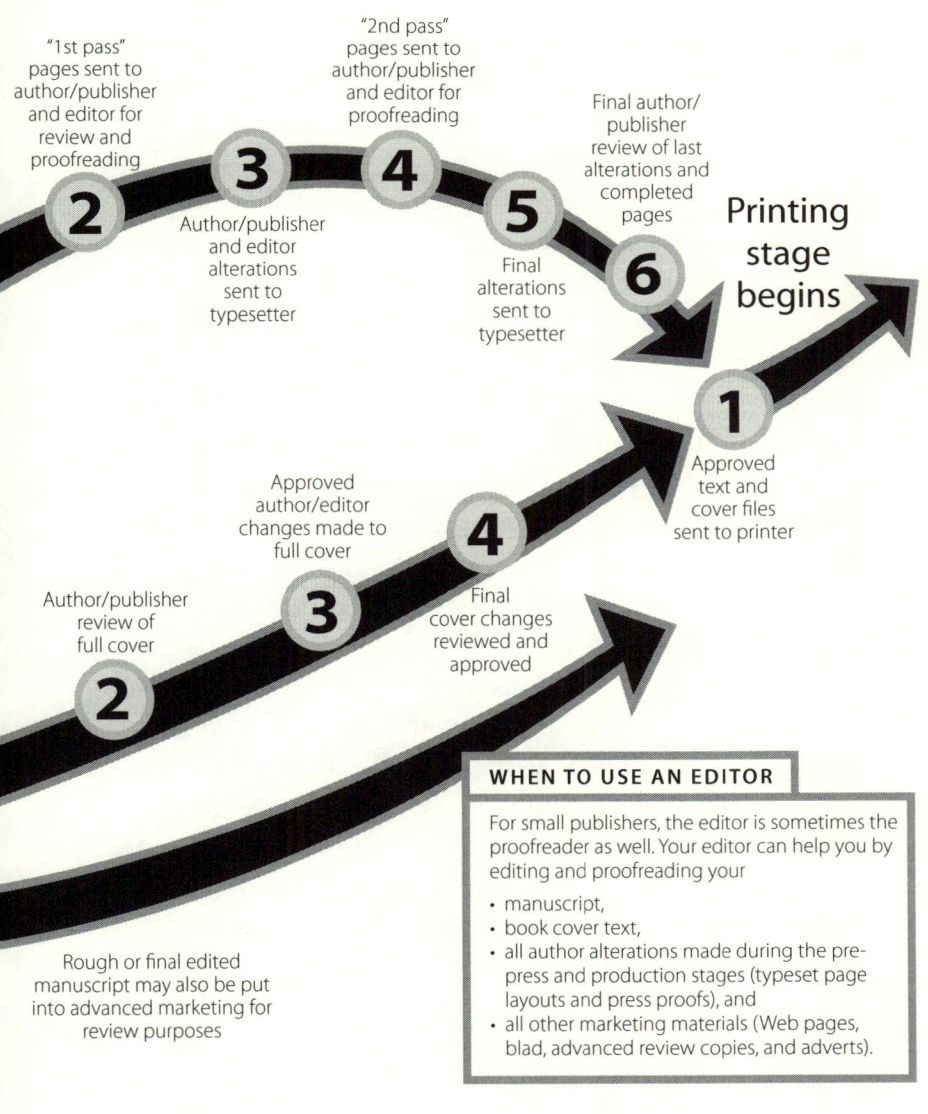

"1st pass" pages sent to author/publisher and editor for review and proofreading

2

3
Author/publisher and editor alterations sent to typesetter

"2nd pass" pages sent to author/publisher and editor for proofreading

4

5
Final alterations sent to typesetter

Final author/ publisher review of last alterations and completed pages

6

Printing stage begins

1
Approved text and cover files sent to printer

Approved author/editor changes made to full cover

4

3

Final cover changes reviewed and approved

Author/publisher review of full cover

2

Rough or final edited manuscript may also be put into advanced marketing for review purposes

WHEN TO USE AN EDITOR

For small publishers, the editor is sometimes the proofreader as well. Your editor can help you by editing and proofreading your

- manuscript,
- book cover text,
- all author alterations made during the pre-press and production stages (typeset page layouts and press proofs), and
- all other marketing materials (Web pages, blad, advanced review copies, and adverts).

or rounds, of revisions at the typeset phase. A first pass (the first typeset pages) might be marked with hundreds or more corrections, the second pass with another 50, the third pass with 10 or so, until the final corrections are made and the book goes to the printer. This back-and-forth process can add a week or two to the schedule at the copyedit stage and another week or two at the typeset stage—usually because everyone is also working on other projects at the same time.

As a self-publishing author, you don't have to consent to every change an editor recommends. You can veto unwelcome changes. But negotiating each change usually isn't worthwhile. If it's not really important, the best practice is to accept the editor's judgment and move on. There are definitely bad editors who want to needlessly rewrite other people's books, but good editors can save your reputation. It's best to take their professional advice—be detached, learn to compromise, and move on so that the project gets done.

How long will the copyediting process take? A 360-page manuscript, for example, (double-spaced, 1-inch margins, roughly 250–300 words per page or around 100,000 words total) may take an experienced editor 1 to 2 weeks to complete, plus 8 to 16 hours of work for the author to review and incorporate the changes from the copyedit. A more complicated manuscript of the same size may take longer and another week may be needed for a second round if the author makes substantial changes that they want the copy editor to review again. A book that has a developmental edit before the copyedit will need at least several weeks added for that stage.

These time estimates are very rough and don't include any time spent checking the manuscript after it is typeset, or what is often seen as the proofreading stage. Closely related to the

PROOFREADING MANUSCRIPTS

Below are some basic proofreading tips and suggestions. Different projects have different requirements. This is not a comprehensive list. Proofreading is best left to a professional, but you may want to do some basic checks, such as the ones listed below, to reduce your editorial proofreading costs and to ensure that your manuscript is in top form even before sending it to an editor.

- Go slow—read the manuscript aloud once and then silently.
- Use but don't rely solely on a spellcheck program.
- Go over the text backwards to check for spelling.
- Create a list of items that need to be checked, and check each item separately. Don't try to check for everything in one proofread of the pages.
- Create a list of book features so that each element can be thoroughly checked for accuracy.

► Grammar, spelling, and accuracy checks

☐ Check general spelling.

☐ Check the spelling of names.

☐ Check the headings for spelling.

☐ Check references and bibliographic entries for style consistency.

☐ Check references and bibliographic entries for factual accuracy.

☐ Check that phone numbers work properly.

☐ Check addresses for accuracy.

☐ Check that URLs work properly and have no line-break hyphens.

☐ Check that art is credited correctly.

☐ Check that pictures have the correct captions.

► Cross-reference checks

☐ Check that chapter titles match the wording in the table of contents and in any chapter references in other chapters and in any running heads.

☐ Check that figure numbers match references in the text.

See the Proofreading Page Layouts Checklist on page 141 for additional proofreading tips and suggestions for after the book is typeset and the page layouts are completed.

editorial process is the process of proofreading (which may also be done by your editor), which will also be discussed in Chapter 7, *The Mysteries of Prepress Book Production Explained*. Editing and proofreading take time and will perhaps test your patience more than any other aspect of the publishing process, especially if you have written a complicated book or one that needs a developmental edit.

WHEN TO SUBMIT YOUR MANUSCRIPT FOR PAGE DESIGN

The primary editing of your manuscript should occur before submitting the manuscript for typesetting. However, you can—and many publishers do—submit the manuscript (complete or in part) for page design prior to final editing. This is done once the actual manuscript is far enough along that all the likely elements have already been used and can be identified—elements such as chapter titles, subtitles, and sidebars. That is, before the final edits are completed, sample sections or a draft copy of the manuscript are sent to a designer to work with to create the design, but not to typeset the whole book yet.

At least one example of each element in the manuscript is flagged, and the designer is instructed to design sample pages—usually the book's front matter, a sample chapter, a few pages that will include any unique or common elements that appear elsewhere in the book, and a few pages with the back matter elements. Once the design options are ready, they are sent to the publisher for review. Some changes may be requested, and, after a back-and-forth process, a final design approved. This way, the page design can be created and approved while the book is being edited.

Once the manuscript is edited, it is delivered to the designer, who will then put it in the approved design. Likewise, it is common for publishers to create a cover design long before a book is edited. This allows publishers to shorten the production time for a book and start early marketing. See Chapter 6, *Book Design that Adds Value* for more about when to start the cover design process.

Therefore, even though the editing process may take longer than you would like (since you feel you have finished writing the book already), both editing and designing can be taking place at the same time (and your review of both). A lot of value is actually being added to your book during this time.

SEEK EXCELLENCE, NOT PERFECTION

Be careful about being too much of an editorial perfectionist, as you may end up never getting published. Few manuscripts are truly perfect, and for that reason publishers created errata and revised editions. *Errata* (plural of erratum) are a list of errors (*corrigenda*). These errors and corrections are printed on a separate page that is inserted in the printed book or printed in later reprints of the book. Errata alert readers to known errors.

Errata are used mostly in technical books and mainly in cases of citations or data that needs to be corrected, rather than in matters of grammar or punctuation. Also, after a book has been in print for a few years, an author may find it desirable to revise the book with new information and issue a new edition. When a new edition is issued, the small errors or grammar details that escaped your editor in the previous edition can be fixed.

PROTECT YOUR CREATIVE EXPRESSION

In the case of copy editors, disputes about who owns the final edited work are unlikely. But the more others become involved with your work, the more the line between editor and contributor can become blurred.

Whenever you work with an editor, it is important to have a written agreement, and you may be the one who has to provide it. Not all freelance editors have contracts because many are used to signing agreements supplied by publishers.

Tip If you don't hire an attorney, you should still have a written agreement. Always create a paper trail even if it consists of e-mails restating the points of discussion and agreed-upon terms. Save your files and e-mails. It may be years later that you need them.

Even if the editor supplies the paperwork, it is wise to consult an intellectual property rights attorney. There are some good books on publishing contracts and affordable online providers of legal contracts. But to a certain degree, you must not assume that what you read or hear with regard to legal matters will allow you to write your own agreement or modify someone else's. Writing your own terms is problematic because intellectual property rights law is continually changing and laws and pending legislation can differ from state to state.

That said, you should always have some form of agreement that includes a confidentiality or non-disclosure clause, provisions outlining who owns and has rights to the final edited manuscript, the terms of payment, terms of delivery (when, how), the composer's representations and warranties, and the governing law for dispute resolution. If you cannot afford an attorney, you should still have a written agreement and always create a paper trail, even if it consists of e-mails restating the points of discussion and agreed-upon terms. Save all your files. It may be years later that you need them.

GETTING THE MOST FROM YOUR EDITOR

Once you find an editor you like, you will probably want to work with them again. Finding a good editor can be difficult, and even after your book is edited, it is useful to have an editor look over whatever else you write for your book's Web site and marketing materials. A second set of eyes and a second opinion is always helpful. Keep your editor happy and recommend him or her whenever you can.

6

Book Design
that Adds Value

How important is design? The cliché "you shouldn't judge a book by its cover" wouldn't exist were it not common for people to do exactly that. In fact, it is much worse than one might imagine. Design is essential in winning acceptance and projecting credibility, and sometimes may determine whether you get any distribution at all.

Book sales agents cannot be expected to read the many books they choose to carry, and most distributors can only afford to display the cover image. In the bookshops, the only visible presence your book may have is the spine, unless the cover is so interesting and appealing that the bookshops choose to give it special display space.

Put simply, it is the book cover that largely determines what books are carried around by sales representatives and displayed in bookshops and in their advertising. It is the cover that gets the most oxygen—*not* what's in the book! For most books, the actual writing is never reviewed, and even if reviewed, there is no way to be sure that the review will have been read by the people who see the book in a bookshop. This is why distributors reject more books because of the cover design than for any other reason.

Tip Distributors reject books more because of the cover design than for any other reason.

Even though book design or package design is the most important factor in the success of many titles, it is sometimes the most neglected detail in the "how-to" world of self-publishing. This is not particularly surprising, since professional book design is not a costly aspect of the publishing budget, especially when compared with marketing costs. That said, product-packaging design, including books, is so important to our fashion-conscious consumer world that billions are spent on it every year. In the world of professional publishing, design is increasingly important to success.

IT'S NOT JUST ABOUT LOOKING "GOOD"

The world is very competitive, and to succeed you need design that goes beyond merely *looking* professional. In affluent consumer societies, design and fashion directly impact purchasing decisions. Skilled designers are professionals who understand design as it relates to commerce. Designers can, for example, take any subject, from politics to the environment, from dieting to religion, and dress it up in the most appealing, or least appealing, visual fashion of the day. When you think of design and aesthetics, think of it as a power that helps you shape perceptions.

- The design can influence your product's perceived value. You can, for example, make it appear more elite and premium, or more like the ultimate high-value bargain.
- The design can differentiate your product from the competition, for example, to make it appear more authoritative and trustworthy, more interesting and exciting, and so on.
- The design can stimulate consumer desire. You can, for example, persuade potential buyers that owning your product reinforces who they are and enhances their status in the eyes of other consumers.

The potential for design to affect your product is real, and it can be utilized to get results. Good design has identifiable traits with direct benefits. A good design will

- fit the sensibilities of its intended audience,
- look contemporary and up-to-date,
- meet professional production standards, and
- stand apart from the competition, or, if desirable, mirror desirable features of the competition to show that you're in the same league.

Having a book design that is audience-appropriate means that the buyer will recognize for whom the book is intended and be more easily assured that it will fulfill expectations. If the audience is men, then a design that is overly feminine may be off-putting. If the audience is young readers, then the design must appeal to their fashion sensibilities. A design that is up-to-date helps a book's perceived value. If a book looks dated, it may be perceived as less valuable because of potentially obsolescent content. If the book looks amateurish,

A book's design can involve a number of considerations, such as how a book will be marketed, the intended audience and how the actual content will be used, the brand image of the author and/or publisher, the design of competing titles, and so on.

it will be perceived as lacking in credibility.

When a book looks too much like other books, the design itself will not add any perceived value over the competition, and it will be evaluated on other criteria.

If the competition is using dated designs or designs that are lacking in novelty and distinction, then you have an opportunity to introduce a fresh design that makes your product stand apart and get more attention. You may also have an opportunity to beat the competition by being the first to add design features such as color text elements, trendier photos, cool diagrams, and so on.

> **Tip** Good design is often critical to marketing success. It can add value to the book, making it easier to use, more fashionable, and more attractive to particular markets.

Many books are bought as gifts. Likewise, readers carry what they read in public places and display their books at home and at work. Having an attractive design will encourage consumers to purchase your book and even use it as an accessory.

There are instances of successful books with amateurish-looking designs, but it would be a mistake to take this to mean that design isn't important. Usually such best-seller success stories occur because of unexpected publicity that is beyond the reach of most publishers' or authors' budgets. In some cases, the book succeeds because it is a new topic that is under-served, that is, there are few other options for consumers. Such books would have sold well no matter how they were packaged. Very few authors can count on

More often than not, the typical self-published book is recognizably self-published simply because of deficiencies in design. The collection of books above includes books designed for large and small publishers, businesses, and self-publishing authors. Self-published books can be designed as well as any other books and can be indistinguishable in design quality.

consumer demand being so great and alternative choices being so limited that his or her book will sell regardless of how it is designed.

PRICING FOR DESIGN SERVICES

Since design is so important and one of the least expensive parts of the publishing budget, it doesn't make sense to sacrifice quality to save money. If you search around, you will notice that prices can vary significantly. Some designers want 3–5 times what others may ask. Some may work for as little as a few hundred dollars, while others require 1–3 thousand dollars for the cover design alone. The most expensive designers are not necessarily the best or the most suited for your particular needs, but the least expensive designers may be risky and end up costing you more.

The best approach is always to check around and look at different designer portfolios. In the world of design, it's not diplomas, but portfolios, that are important. What matters is not where he or she went to school, but what they have done and can do. In the cases where you can observe portfolios (not all designers have examples they are willing to show), there are often dramatic differences in quality and style. Always see examples, and let quality be your guide. See what they have done, and pick the best designer who can give you what you want for the budget you have—rather than simply the cheapest designer you can find.

Tip — Check around and look at different designers' work. In the world of publishing, portfolios are more important than diplomas.

What do you get for your money? Typically, a book designer will start by providing consultation and design options. These options may be supplied in the form of PDFs or JPEG images that you can view on your computer, or they may send you actual digital printouts. You can then pick one of these options, or elements from several options, as well as request other changes. The contract may stipulate a limited number of revisions (usually 3) that you can request, but designers will often exceed that number to get the desired result and please the client. The revision limitation is there

Typically, the designer will provide 2–3 distinctly different design options for the front cover. You may then need to request revisions, to see elements combined from the several designs, or to see how one or more of the designs will look with different photos, typography, or colors. These cover designs were commissioned by The American Institute of Architects.

Laminates, varnishes, foils, embossing, and die-cuts are all increasingly common features used to make books stand apart from competitors. Book design is, however, open to an almost endless range of possibilities. For the design shown above left, the cover folds around and can be held closed by a magnet or by an attached elastic red band. The compass can be an image or a real compass embedded into the cover. The covers can be pseudo-leather, or an image of leather adhered to the artboard with a soft filling in between. If such options are within your production budget, let your designer know that you are interested in design options that make your product distinctive. These cover designs were commissioned by Ben-Bella Books.

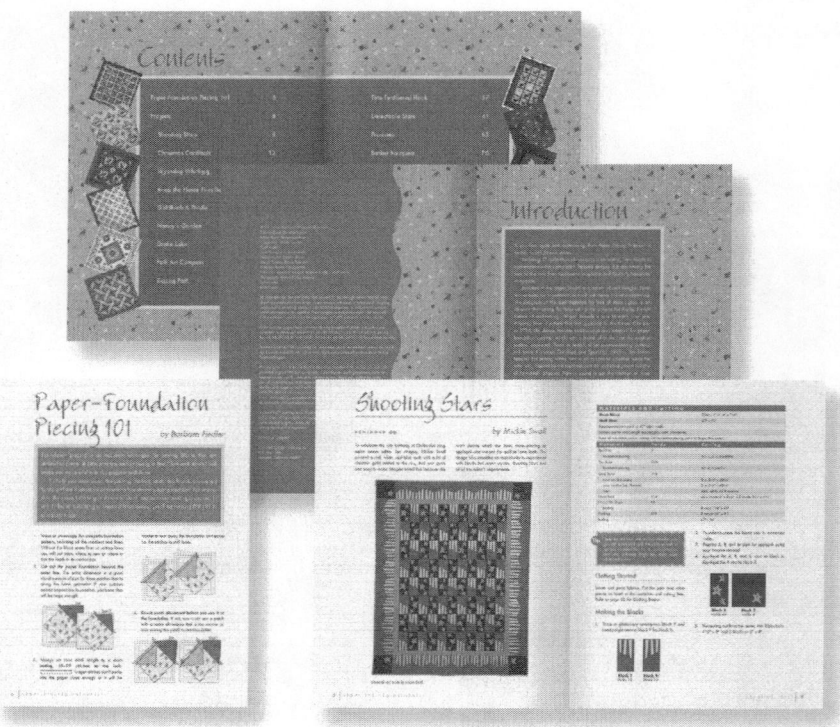

With effective developmental editing, complex books (like the quilting book above by C&T Publishing) can be designed so that they are appealing and user-friendly resources. Good developmental editing helps the design process add perceptible value to books that contain technical information.

When I designed *Boating Skills and Seamanship*, along with the companion *Sailing Skills and Seamanship*, for the United States Coast Guard Auxiliary (published by International Marine of McGraw-Hill), my goal was to create a clean functional design with broad and long-lasting appeal. The design employs visual navigation in the form of chapter opener photos repeated in the table of contents and color-coordinated information categories, such as boxed chapter objectives, end-chapter quizzes, warnings, tips, etc. The red, white, and blue colors reinforce the brand image for the United States Coast Guard Auxiliary, and to reflect the nautical content, the running head page graphics are designed to suggest keels.

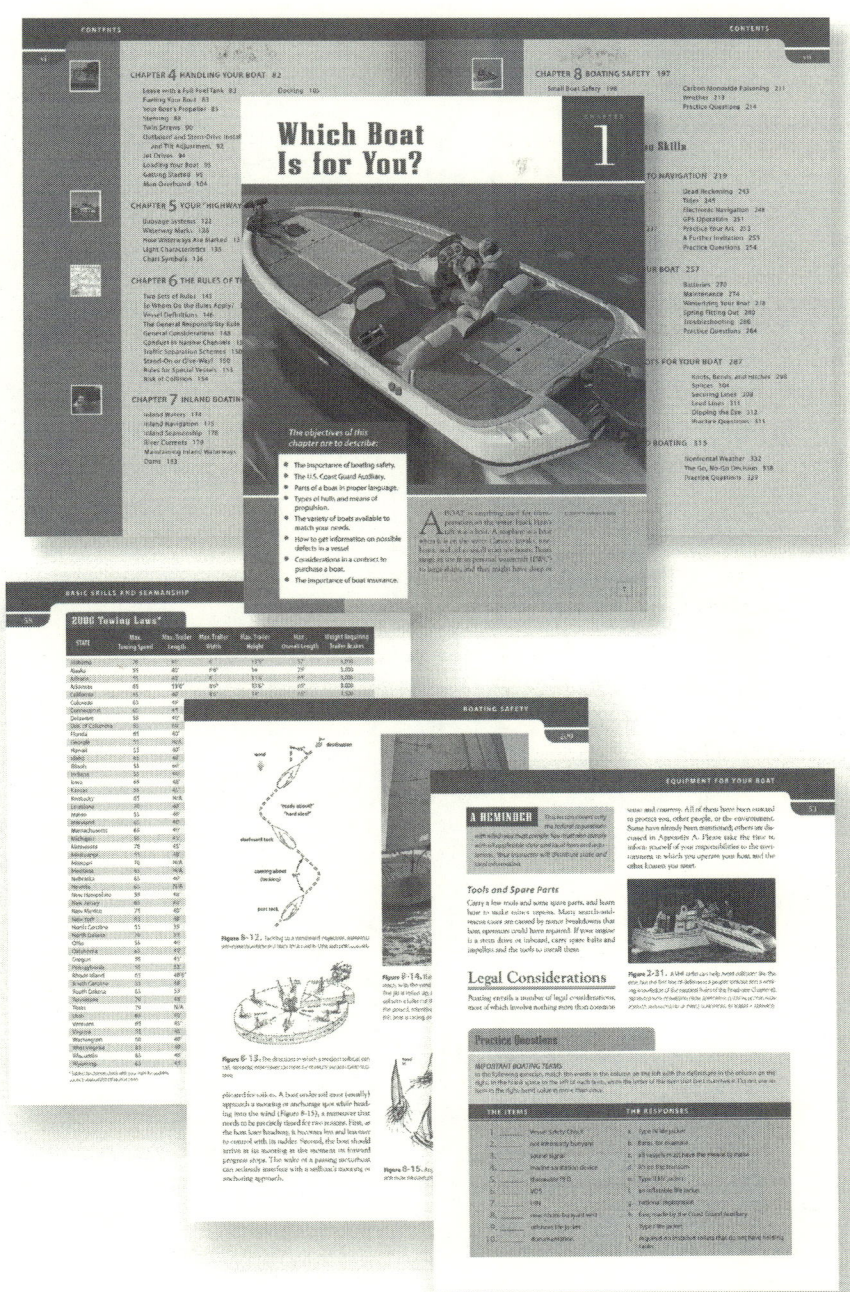

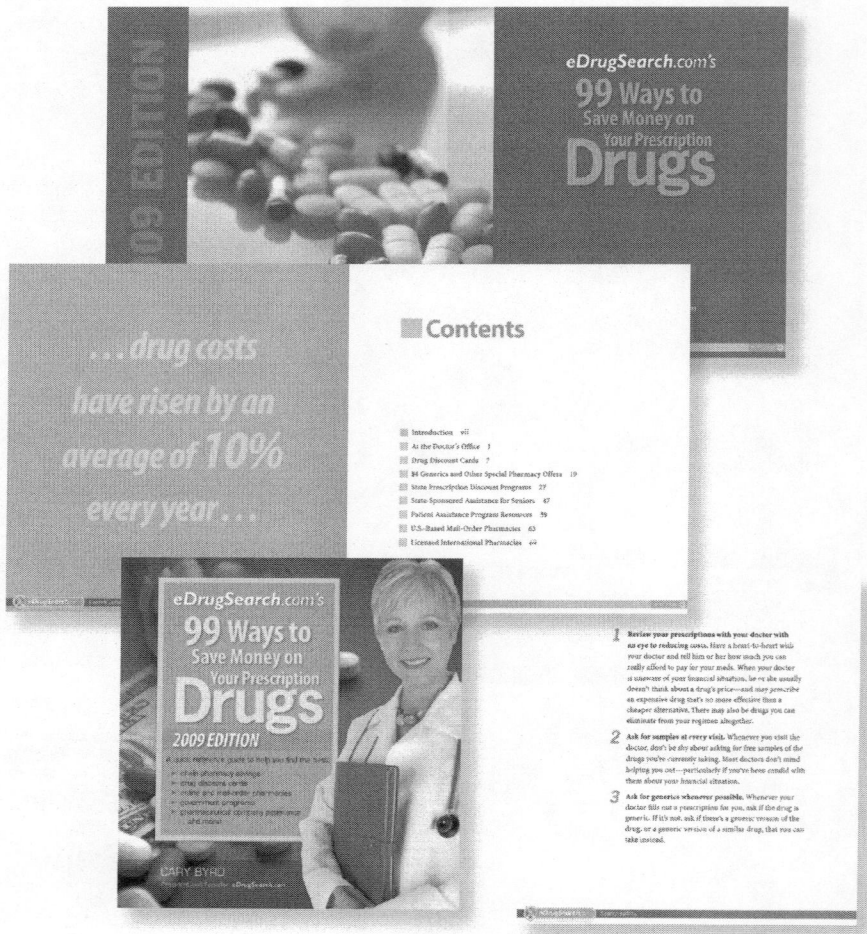

e-Books offer benefits, features, and design possibilities that are unique, such as hyperlinked content and navigation, no upfront printing expenses, no page-count limitations, instant worldwide distribution, security features, and more. Books that were once cost-restricted to black and white, can be published in full color. Photos only need to be 72 ppi at the size placed, making image content more affordable than for process printing—depending on the terms of the stock provider's license agreement. The design examples shown here (for edrugsearch.com and photopreneur. com) include a facing-page design and non-facing–page designs.

> **Tip** Know what's in your contract. The primary task of a designer is to create the look for the book, not necessarily the files that will go to the printer.

to protect the designer from excessive changes from clients who can't make up their minds unless they have seen and ruled out every color or font option possible. If you have trouble deciding and want more options, expect that the extra work will involve additional fees, usually billed at an hourly rate. Most designers have a good idea of how long it will take and will either offer a flat fee or an hourly rate, sometimes stating the expected number of hours.

Design is not the same as typesetting, page layout, or press-ready file production. The task of the designer is to create the look for the book, but not necessarily the files that will go to the printers. Most *book* designers can do cover and interior designs, page layout, and create press-ready files, but if it's not in the contract, don't assume you are getting those services. Graphic designers who are not book designers usually don't have the necessary skills to perform such tasks. It's okay to use a designer for a book cover and then give the design to someone else to do the final file production, but it's usually more efficient to hire a designer who can do both. More about making designs press-ready will be explained in Chapter 7, *The Mysteries of Prepress Book Production Explained.*

TIPS FOR SELECTING A DESIGNER

If you decide to hire a professional designer for your book, it is worth keeping in mind that in this age of desktop com-

For this book, I worked as both designer and illustrator. The book presents life in the Pacific Northwest forestry industry. The hand-colored woodcut illustrations and interior graphics were intended to appeal to Northwest readers and to reflect the contemporary sensibilities of the author and publisher. Design, like a favorable book review, is important to a book's success, but in this case the success of the design was also evident in the review: *"I'm going to break with tradition and start this column with a word of praise for the top-notch design of* Overstory: Zero" *. . . Designer/illustrator Michael Rohani's work is a pleasure to look at and to hold."* (book reviewer Barbara Lloyd McMichael in *The Oregonian*)

puting many people consider themselves graphic designers simply because they own design software and think they have great taste. There are also numerous art and design schools that churn out would-be designers every year, but these students lack experience and some lack natural talent, too. Finding a good designer with the level of experience required to handle book projects can require some searching.

Most design studios do not serve publishers or book projects because other types of package and advertising design are more profitable. So even if you hire a professional graphic design studio, you cannot assume they understand book production requirements. Ask to see what *book* projects they have done.

Many printers offer very-low-cost design services, and while they may have a great deal of experience with printing books, it is not generally the case that printers have staff that will produce good design for books or anything else. Some printers may have on hand nicely designed books that were designed by someone else. If you hire a printer to do design, make sure you are really getting the designer who did the examples you like.

There are also some design studios that offer design services for publishers, and, in some cases, these studios are also willing to work with self-publishing authors. These studios are likely to understand publishing industry fashions, the workflow of books, and issues involved in different book printing processes. They can ensure that once the files are prepared they actually print as intended.

If you use a design studio that specializes in books or a freelancer who has experience with books, you may be able to reduce your project management time and costs. Some designers who are not familiar with books may do the design, but outsource the actual prepress production. It is possible to end up with a cover designer and a page designer, a person doing the cover mechanical, and someone else doing the typesetting and page layout. The printer is then left trying to make the files work. This is not always a problem, but it can be, especially if the designers are using different software. Publishers sometimes use multiple suppliers when it provides cost-cutting opportunities, but it requires having an art director or manager who can coordinate the suppliers and keep track of the schedule.

Smaller design studios that specialize in books can usually do all the necessary tasks, and that will reduce your project management requirements and costs. Another benefit of using a design studio that specializes in books will become apparent when it's time to select a printer. Not all printers do books, and design studios that specialize in books will have better knowledge about printers that can.

You can also outsource to a different country to take advantage of favorable wage and exchange rates, but be aware that this works best for prepress production services and for printing, rather than for design, which is more sensitive to cultural differences. To protect yourself against fraud or incompetence, get referrals from the supplier's clients who reside in the country where you live.

DESIGNER AND ARTIST CONTRACTS

Anytime you work with artists, whether writers, designers, illustrators, or photographers, it is essential to have a written contract that addresses issues such as usage rights and other expectations. Professional designers will have their own contracts, but you should not feel obliged to sign anyone's contract without negotiating additional terms or changes if they are needed. The contract should specify the work covered by the estimate. Extras, such as shipping or proofreading, are unlikely to be included, so keep in mind the possibility of additional costs.

> **Tip** If you get artwork from an artist, a cousin, or friend without a contract, it may come back to bite you later, especially if your book is successful.

Most designers will want payment in thirds, one-third before starting the project and the final third upon delivery or 30 days after delivery. You can also expect to see a collection clause.

Most contracts will include an indemnity clause that protects the designer against legal action that might result from materials provided by the author that turn out to infringe on the rights of someone else. Also, either in the contract or separately, most designers will have you agree that you are solely responsible for checking the files before printing occurs.

Some contracts will have a clause that grants the designer the right to use the design in their own portfolio or promotional materials (a good sign that they take pride in the work they do).

Don't expect designers or other artists to give you complete ownership, which is rarely needed and never automatically granted unless it is spelled out in the correct legal language in a written contract. Creative professionals—designers, photographers, illustrators—usually charge more based on the degree to which they are giving up the ownership of their creations. In such cases, it is only necessary to purchase what you need. The contract should state for what purpose the design will be used and the price covered by that usage.

Creating a book design will likely involve you in a number of service and license agreements. If, for example, you buy a royalty-free photograph for your book cover, you may be purchasing the right to use it forever on that book cover. This is not, however, the same as complete ownership. The stock photo provider is not, for example, allowing you to resell the image to other users. The license agreement is only with you. You could commission a photographer to take the photograph you desire under an agreement that gives you exclusive rights and perpetual ownership, and an explicit provision allowing you to even sell the photograph to other users on coffee mugs and t-shirts, but this would likely cost much more and be totally unnecessary for your book-publishing purposes. Similarly, a designer may grant a license in the contract that you can use the design for that title for as long as you wish and for as many reprints as you wish, but, again, this is not the same as having the right to use the design for other books or to sell it to other authors. The better the designer, the more likely they are to be careful about such matters, and your insisting needlessly on full ownership may result in paying for usage that you don't need.

One method of getting complete ownership is to insist that the designer/artist sign a *work for hire* or *work made for*

Tip Contrary to popular belief, *royalty-free* doesn't mean you can use it any way you want. Many RF license agreements include restrictions.

hire contract. This legal terminology means (in some cases) that for the purposes of the work covered in the contract, the designer/artist is effectively your employee and you own fully whatever work they create. Legal definitions and the provisions of the law, however, differ between states and countries. Using this type of language in a contract may potentially subject you to employer liability and insurance issues.

Even if you get an attorney to draft work made for hire language, some designers simply refuse to sign such contracts. Other designers treat work made for hire agreements as "buy-outs," a term used to refer to a higher purchase fee for complete usage rights. They may, for example, agree to the work for hire clause, but at double or more above the standard usage fee they normally charge. Most professional designers view such contracts as unethical because the client is seen as trying to take advantage of the designer. This is because, under the *work made for hire* arrangement, the client can buy something at the price set for one type of usage and then use it for other purposes that are worth more.

As an alternative to the typical usage fees and license agreements of designers, you can hunt down the services of an amateur willing to do it for less or nothing, but this may expose you to risks and new problems that end up spoiling the project. Working with designers who, for example, are not careful about license issues when it comes to their own work, may mean they are unaware of such issues when it comes to how they use art, photos, and font software when creating a design for you. If you get artwork *without a contract* from an artist, a cousin, or a friend, it may come back to bite you later, even if your book isn't very successful.

The costs of professional book design are too low to be worth all these risks. It's best to simply hire a talented professional who understands intellectual property rights and states clearly what you are paying for, so you pay only for what you need.

THE DESIGN BRIEF

Once you select a designer, you need to provide him or her with some understanding of your needs and expectations. To do this, you'll need to provide a *design brief*. The goal of the design brief is to facilitate the book design process and ensure that you receive a design that helps your book sell. Or put another way, the brief will help you to make sure that once the design work is done, it is something you can use.

If you allow a designer to start designing without a brief—creating anything he or she wants—you may use up your design budget before you get what you need. Instead, prepare a design brief (see The Design Brief Checklist on page 118). It can be delivered over the phone or in person, but it is usually best to outline the essentials in writing so the designer can refer to it. If a designer wastes time straying too far from the brief, going back over the original design brief should prevent you having to pay additional fees to get the project back on track.

Avoid being overly specific. Don't limit the designer's creativity and originality. In many cases, you'll have three options from the designer, but give the designer enough freedom to provide at least one option that is purely the designer's own suggestion. How much or how little direction you should provide depends on the ability of the designer,

DESIGN BRIEF CHECKLIST

Provide the book designer with a short design brief. A design brief will help facilitate the book design process and ensure that you receive a design that fits your project needs. The design brief should include a description of the project and any resources that you have that can be useful in the process.

► *A project description*

☐ A description of physical attributes: This should include title, size, any text that will appear on the cover (bullet lists, cover endorsements, awards), interior text elements, and the anticipated page count).

☐ Any information about the final book that is influenced by the budget or publishing method, such as whether it can be full-color or if there are constraints against color or special printing processes and whether the book will be published as an e-book, or using a print-on-demand or process printing, or all three methods.

☐ Design objectives: A brief description of the *unique selling proposition* (USP) or the *high concept* that needs to be communicated and the intended audience. If you have a book proposal describing what the book is about and what audience it is intended for, its benefits, etc., key attributes, then you can excerpt material from it to use as art direction for the designer.

► *Resources:*

☐ Include your contact information.

☐ Include any necessary art (any art or photographs that will be used in the book).

☐ Your publisher identity resources: Your logo file and, if you have one, your publisher *identity manual*. An identity manual is any style guidelines about your publisher identity, such as how your company image looks in your marketing materials (standardized fonts, colors, graphics, etc.). It often includes your mission statement and company vision.

☐ A manuscript sample: For design purposes, you don't necessarily have to supply the entire manuscript. It is usually sufficient if you supply the front matter pages (especially the title page and table of contents) and a sample chapter with all the main book elements.

☐ Main competitors' samples: It is helpful to give the designer images of your main competitor's book covers and interiors with the objective that you would like your book design to exceed the competition.

but whatever the book designer's level of experience, it is helpful to provide some basic direction.

HOW TO CRITIQUE BOOK DESIGNS

Covers

Once the book designer has provided design options, you will need to evaluate them. This is something you can either do yourself or with the help of a publicist or focus group. An author/publisher can be happy with a cover design only to have their sales representatives and distributors talk them out of it. Always get the opinion of your distributors if you can.

You can solicit opinions by posting the design options on your Web site or e-mailing JPEGs. You can also make a digital printout and put it around any book that it will fit. Set up the mock book in a display with its competitors next to it and ask viewers for opinions, like which one they notice first and prefer most.

In addition to aesthetic issues such as visual impact, novelty, and fashion, there are some practical questions worth keeping in mind during the process of critiquing the book design options. For more things to consider, see the Design Evaluation Checklist on page 120.

Page designs

Have realistic expectations. Good design is more than simply something that looks attractive. Ultimately, good design adds value, but the designer cannot always bring out the full potential of the project if the necessary author/editor manuscript preparation hasn't occurred. In some cases, adding value has to start in the planning and developmental

DESIGN EVALUATION CHECKLIST

Once the designer provides design options, you will need to critique or evaluate them, not merely by the standard of what appeals to you, but based on what works for the intended market, how well it suits the book, how the book will be advertised, and your longer-term publishing goals. Here are a few questions to consider:

► *Cover designs*

☐ How well does the cover convey the main unique selling proposition and high concept of the book? If it's a how-to book, does the cover communicate the topic, features, and benefits offered by the book?

☐ How well will the cover design look when it is reduced to the size of a postage stamp in a book catalog, online retailer Web site, or magazine ad?

☐ How well will the book cover design compare when it is placed next to competitor titles? Does it stand out? Is it iconic? Is it memorable, and would anyone want to share it or display it? The book with the best design in the category may be the most successful. When a book is self-published, it must still look like it was published by a professional publisher and intended for booksellers and for the buying public.

☐ How will the design appeal to the target audience? Will they identify with it?

☐ Can the design be adapted to a series design?

► *Interior designs*

☐ How well does the interior page layout convey the unique features and benefits of the book?

☐ Is the interior design reader-friendly? This means more than type large enough to be read. It can mean, for example, an open design with sidebars and pull quotes and other elements that enable the consumer to use or benefit from the contents more easily and without reading the entire book.

☐ Will the book design—format or trim size, and page count—easily convert to the different publication methods:, process printing, print-on-demand, and e-book formats?

The designer may supply page samples with crop marks visible (like the ones shown on page 126). Always get PDFs of the samples with and without crop marks to better view margin sizes, and always print out pages at 100% and then trim at the crop marks to accurately view the actual page and margin dimensions.

stage—before the author files are delivered to the designer. It's not, after all, the designer's job to reorganize material in your book or to find text that can be put into interesting features like sidebars, pull quotes, review questions, etc. If you, the author, or your editor indicates specifically what texts belongs in what type of element, then, yes, the designer can identify and transform the text into appealing book features to make the book easier to use and navigate.

When done right, the design can become a major influence in the decision of potential readers to purchase the book. A travel book, for example, that includes maps with recommended walking routes, restaurant reviews, and other useful features will be more appealing than a book with the same material only described in words. These kinds of design features are becoming more common in more types of books because they *add value* by enabling readers to benefit from the content more quickly and efficiently. The pull quotes and sidebar features that are characteristic of many successful magazine designs are now being used to make books more appealing. Some designers may be willing to give you suggestions, but, ultimately, it is the author and editor who are responsible for the kind of developmental editing and manuscript preparation necessary for such types of books.

Finally, when you request design changes, be diplomatic. Compliment what you like about the design, before offering

> **Tip** Start the design process before you have finished the final editing. The sooner you can use the cover design for marketing, the better.

criticism—but never hold back. Professional designers expect criticism, and they expect clients to request changes. Designers who work with professional publishers are used to long lists of changes and will simply make the changes and move forward.

If you hire a good designer, you will likely get good design options to choose from. That said, be aware that even though your requested changes may "ruin" a design in the opinion of the designer, he or she may not let you know. Professional designers are not likely to tell you that your ideas suck—even when it's true. Just because a designer does what you request, don't take it to mean that he or she agrees with you.

Most professional designers are not trying to create purely for self-expression. Artists of that sort are too annoying to clients to last long in the business. Most book designers will be more concerned with giving you, the client, what you want (good or bad), so that he or she can complete the job on time, collect the fee, and encourage you to come back with more projects. If you trust the designer and really want an honest opinion, be sure to ask for it, but otherwise don't expect the designer to argue with you in order to prevent you from spoiling the design.

In addition to possible referrals, most designers are looking for good examples to put in their portfolios to help them get more work. Professional designers are motivated to provide good work.

WHEN TO START THE COVER DESIGN PROCESS

Once a book's title and concept are reasonably established, publishers will get a designer to start designing the front cover (see editorial workflow diagram on pages 88–89).

Individual self-publishing authors can do things in the same way. Once the cover is ready, it can be used in pre-publication marketing. It may appear on the publisher and/or author Web site, in catalogs, and in other advertising. Because catalogs take time to design, lay out, and print, especially if the printing is outsourced to a different country, publishers begin this process as soon as possible. A self-publishing author may not be concerned with a catalog, but may find it useful to have the cover design in advance of publication for other purposes, such as a Web site or direct mail or e-mail postcard campaign.

> **Tip** Have the cover design created early so you can test it with colleagues and potential readers, and if the reaction is unfavorable get it revised or a new one before printing it.

Having the cover created early also allows the author to test the design with colleagues and potential readers, and if the reaction is unfavorable get it revised or a new one. You can use inexpensive digital printing for samples before printing thousands of copies with process printing.

The first two important opportunities you have to market your book are 1) the announcement that the book is forthcoming and 2) the announcement that it is now available. If you wait until the book is published to start marketing, it will already be old by the time word starts getting around. With new titles appearing each season, reviewers are less interested in old books. To escape this difficulty, you should get the cover design ready at the earliest possible date. A good cover design is the first and best way to communicate that the book is a reality and something people should be interested in buying.

Similarly, some publishers start the page design process once the actual manuscript is far enough along that all the likely elements can be identified, as discussed earlier on page 94. This also helps with advance marketing. At the same time the book is being designed, the manuscript is usually being edited, and once it receives its final edits it is then sent without delay to the designer or typesetter to typeset and lay out all the pages according to the already approved design specifications. Once the first set of pages is ready, many publishers create *blads* and/or *advance review copies* (ARCs). Blads are small booklet samples of the book that usually list the publisher's marketing plans on the back. Blads have the working book cover on the front, a table of contents, a book description, and a text sample from the book. The purpose of the blad is to convince book distributors and sellers that the book is interesting and will be advertised enough that they can expect sales. If you are doing all the marketing and distribution, you may not need a blad. An ARC is a sample of the complete pages for distribution to potential book reviewers and/or specialists who might be willing to review or endorse the book before it is printed. Excerpts from qualified reviewers can be added to the cover or to front matter pages.

More about marketing will be presented in *Book Marketing Essentials.*

GETTING THE MOST FROM YOUR DESIGNER

Once you hire a designer—as with your editor, printer, and marketing professionals—be aware that sustaining this relationship can have many long-term benefits. This is especially true during the main period of time it takes to design and market a book.

You will likely have many design needs or reasons to get back with the designer beyond simply getting a cover design. You will need marketing materials and may want more books or future editions designed. Your designer will have all the fonts and software files used to create the book design. The designer will be able to convert elements from these files with accurate color and style matches into other related products and advertising collateral that you can use, such as blads, ARCs, Web sites, landing pages, e-mails, banner ads, fliers, point-of-purchase displays, etc.

When it comes time to choose a printer, bear in mind that a printer has less incentive to do a good job for a one-time self-publishing author, whereas a printer will want to preserve its reputation with the designer or design studio that recommends its services to clients on a regular basis. So if you choose your printer through your designer, they may serve you better.

Living Timelines
FILIPINA/O AMERICAN HISTORY UNIT

3.1

✓ CHECKLIST

Lesson Plan Materials

The Mysteries of Prepress
Book Production Explained

Typically, you (the author/publisher) are the ultimate judge for checking your editor's work, just as the editor checks your work, but it is your editor or proofreader who should have the technical skill to check the typesetting and page layout. It is the designer who should have the skill to check the print proofs provided by the printer. That is, there should always be someone else checking the work of each service provider.

Once you approve the cover and interior design, the files have to be completed and prepared for print. All the steps that are involved in getting the files ready to print are referred to as *prepress production*. This technical and complicated stage of the process involves skills that you shouldn't have to ever know. The people who run publishing companies leave these matters to the experts, and you can do the same. However, the more you know, the better. In this chapter, I will explain some of the basics. Provided you hire experienced book professionals, you can get others to perform all the necessary checks for you. If there are any problems, they will spot them and know how to get them fixed.

Ultimately, you will need to rely on the expert skills and judgments of professionals. Book production is a collaborative process, and, as the author/publisher, you will need to keep open the channels of communication between your editor/proofreader, your designer, and your printer, and any other persons who may be involved in production. With that in mind, you will only need to have some understanding of the basic processes involved in prepress production and the terminology used by the professionals you contract to do the work.

The goal of prepress book production is to get all the texts, graphics, and book elements typeset and positioned on the pages. Every page must be completed in accordance with your approved design and in a way that will print correctly. The photos or art also have to be checked for color mode, file type, and resolution, and prepared for the specific publication method used.

PREPRESS BASICS

After design, prepress production can be divided into three basic processes:

1. Typesetting and layout
2. Proofreading
3. Press-ready file creation

These three processes take place for both the files created for the cover and for the interior pages. Some book projects require other files as well. If, for example, you plan to have special spot varnishes on the cover, or the book title and author name stamped onto a cloth-bound hardback cover, then special files have to be created for each of these features. All files need to be proofread and made print-ready.

Prepress production is everything required to implement the design before the print stage of the project. Print-on-demand (POD) has different prepress production requirements than process printing, and you must inform the designer and anyone working on the files what print methods you will be using, in order to avoid additional costs. In the case of ebooks, the final pre-publication (there is no press involved) includes file size and color optimization and working hyperlinks in the texts. The benefits of these three publications options, and how to plan for all three, are discussed in Chapter 8, *Your Publishing Options: eBooks, Print on Demand, and Process Printing*.

TYPESETTING

Once a page layout sample design is approved and the copyediting is completed, the text is typeset and then fitted to the complete page layouts. Digital typesetting today is often very closely associated with the actual process of page layout. The person who typesets the book will likely be the person who does the page layout. *Typesetting* and *copyfitting* are tasks sometimes performed by different production artists. But today, both can usually be done by the same designer who designed your book, or at least by the same design studio.

Different types of books have different typesetting requirements. If the book designer has not typeset books for publishers that require high standards, such as academic

QUICK GUIDE: BASIC PAGE LAYOUT TERMINOLOGY

The diagrams below show some basic page layout terminology. Books that will be printed using both print-on-demand (POD) and process printing should be designed with text at least ½ to ¾ inches between text and margin trims because POD printing is often less precise.

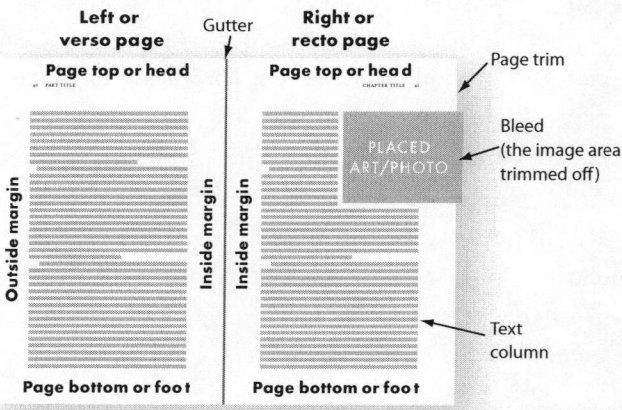

For process printing, pages are set up with "crop marks" at each corner to indicate where the page is trimmed on the outside and folded on the inside. Text too close to the trim can be clipped off. The portion of an image that extends beyond the trim is called a "bleed." A "full bleed" is an image that extends beyond all four edges of the page. Images that bleed need to be large enough to extend at least ⅛ of an inch beyond the intended trim.

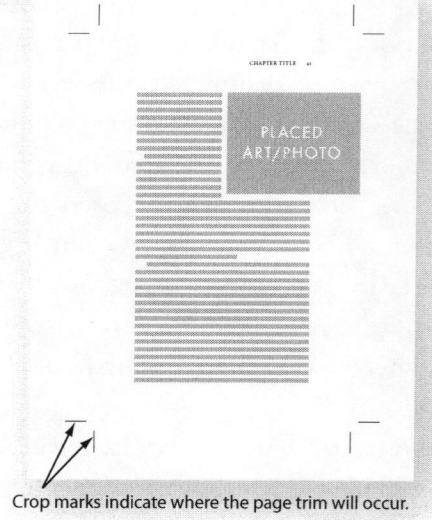

Crop marks indicate where the page trim will occur.

QUICK GUIDE COMMON TYPESETTING ERRORS

The sample page below shows some typical typesetting errors that should not occur and all of which can be fixed. Stacked words, excessive and unnecessary hyphens, widows, orphans, etc., spoil the page composition and make the text more difficult to read.

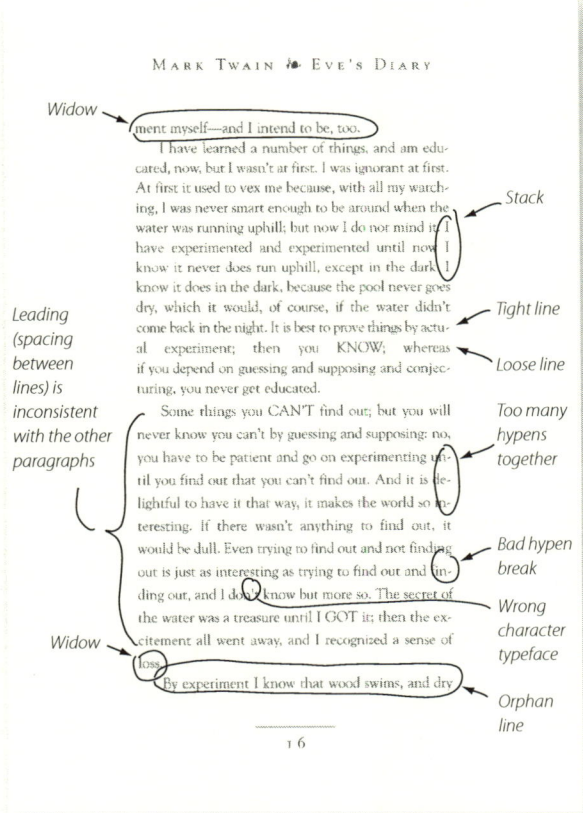

In addition to these errors, all elements throughout a book (running heads, boxed text, footnotes, pull quotes, etc.) should be styled consistently during the page layout stage using your approved design. Style inconsistencies are *layout errors*.

> **Tip** Professional typesetting involves attention to detail. It is not merely a matter of importing the text and letting it flow from page to page in a page layout program.

publishers and university presses, it may be difficult for a novice to ascertain whether they really understand the technical requirements involved for such books. Professional typesetting involves attention to detail. It is not merely a matter of importing the text and letting it flow from page to page in a page layout program. If you want to hire a particular designer who does not do page layout, you will then need to find someone who has the necessary skill to complete the project.

The designer will design the layout and in the process determine the basic specification for the fonts used, line lengths, line spacing (called *leading*, pronounced *ledding*), all text columns, and the margins. The designer may also provide a *cast off* (likely page count produced for the given font size) in order to determine if the book will be too short or too long (given printer specs), meaning that the type specs might need to be changed.

The person who typesets the actual edited text according to the designer's specifications needs to understand typography—issues such as letter spacing, letter weights, ligatures, and kerning. They need to know the correct and incorrect ways of using symbols, small caps, hyphens and dashes, and quotation marks, and possibly the correct way to set fractions and other math, depending on the book's subject matter. How well the type is set can influence the quality of your book, and it is therefore helpful also to have an editor/proofreader with the necessary experience to check the work for you.

It's also useful to have on hand the basic typographic terminology so you can talk more accurately with your designer and copyfitter. For example, it is easier for very young children to read books that use font styles with the letter "a" that looks like this: a. This type of "a" is a *single-story lowercase* letter. Use the typographic Quick Guides in this chapter for reference.

PAGE LAYOUT

Page layout, also called page *composition* or *copyfitting* (as distinct from page design), involves

- fitting the text and graphics into all the approved book design specifications in a consistent way.
- fitting the text on each page for optimum legibility.

Good page layout improves the functionality and perceived value of the book. The quality of the page layout begins with the choices made by the designer for the particular needs of the project and extends to the final fitting of the copy into the approved design. Experienced book designers and page layout artists know that how type is set can determine whether a book fails or succeeds as a product. Type too close to the inner gutter, for example, can be hard to read and cause the reader to put more stress on the binding than it can bear. Text, such as running heads and page numbers, placed too close to the *page trim* can end up being partially trimmed off. Text lines that are too long or too short can make reading difficult.

In addition to design issues, such as the positions of the main text elements, an experienced copyfitter will avoid such errors as loose and/or tight lines, *orphan* and *widow* lines, *rivers*, *stacks*, uneven page columns, bad page breaks, and other typographic and layout problems. The more important the information communicated and the higher the level of formal education among the intended readership, the more critical it is that the book be properly composed. Good page layout involves checking the fit for every line of text in the book! And, every time a change is made, the text must be checked to ensure that there is not a knock-on effect for the text that follows the change (new problems created on the lines following the line you just corrected). Adding a single letter in a page layout program can push text forward causing pages to misalign and text to disappear.

Tip If you hire a designer who is not experienced with books, get the typesetting, layout, and file preparation done by someone who is. It could save you a lot of pain.

There are, in fact, many common problems that go wrong with books in the production stage when designers and/or layout artists are used who are not experienced in books. In some cases, the digital files will even fail to print—not because they cannot be printed, but because they are not set up to print as books. This usually happens because the program was used incorrectly to create the page layouts. In such cases, it may be easier and cheaper to scrap both the design and the page files entirely and to start over. In some cases, files

QUICK GUIDE — TYPOGRAPHIC CHARACTERS

For better communication with your typesetter and editor, it is helpful to refer to characters and symbols by their names.

!	exclam
¡	exclam down
¿	question down
"	quote double left
"	quote double right
'	quote left
'	quote right
»	guillemot right
«	guillemot left
‹	guille single left
›	guille single right
{	brace left
}	brace right
[	square bracket left
]	square bracket right
(	parenthesis left
)	parenthesis right
^	caret or ascii circumflex
—	em-dash
–	en-dash
-	hyphen
_	underscore
&	ampersand
§	section
¶	paragraph
•	bullet
...	ellipsis
©	copyright

®	registered
™	trademark
@	at
*	asterisk
†	dagger
‡	dagger double
/	slash
\	back-slash
/	solidus or fraction
|	bar
°	degree

MATH

%	percent
‰	per thousand
#	number sign
∞	infinity
÷	divide
+	plus
±	plus minus
≠	not equal
≤	less equal
≥	greater to equal
<	lesser
>	greater
¬	logicalnot
′	feet
″	inches
≈	approx. to equal
Δ	delta
∫	integral
◊	lozenge

Ω	Omega
∂	partial diff.
π	pi
µ	mu
√	radical

LIGATURES & DIPHTHONGS

fi	fi
fl	fl
œ	œ
æ	æ

FLOATING ACCENTS/ DIACRITICAL MARKS

´	acute
`	grave accent
ˇ	caron
ˆ	circumflex
~	tilde
¨	dieresis
^	circumflex
¯	macron
˘	breve
˛	ogonek
¸	cedilla
˝	hungarumlaut or double acute accent
à	a grave
á	a acute
â	a circumflex
ã	a tilde
ä	a dieresis

å	aring
ç	c cedilla
è	e grave
é	e acute
ê	e circumflex
ë	e dieresis
ì	i grave
í	i acute
î	i circumflex
ï	i dieresis
ñ	n tilde
ò	o grave
ó	o acute
ô	o circumflex
õ	o tilde
ö	o dieresis
ø	o slash
š	s caron
ù	u grave
ú	u acute
û	u circumflex
ü	u dieresis
ÿ	y dieresis
ß	German double s

CURRENCY SYMBOLS

$	dollar
¢	cent
£	pounds sterling
¥	yen
€	euro
ƒ	floren

QUICK GUIDE | BASIC TYPE TERMINOLOGY

The diagrams below show the basic anatomy of type and the correct terminology to describe it. These terms and techniques are useful to know if and when you ever need to discuss type questions with the designer or typesetter working on your book project.

TYPOGRAPHY AND TYPE ANATOMY

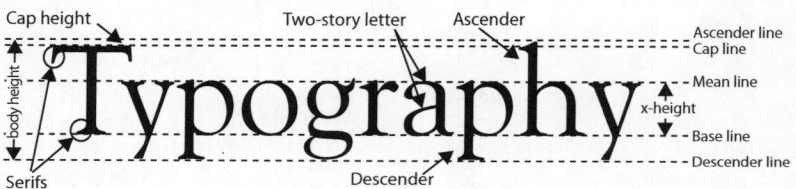

Cap height — Two-story letter — Ascender — Ascender line — Cap line — Mean line — x-height — Base line — Descender line — body height — Serifs — Descender

x-Height is literally the height of the lower case letter "x" in a typeface, or the portion of all letters not including either the ascender of "h,k,l" or descenders of "g,p,y."

As these examples show, it is the x-height of the typeface that determines its visual impact more than its point size.

Age — 24-point Perpetua
Age — 24-point Goudy
Age — 24-point Myriad
Age — 24-point Nuptial

24 pt

Ligatures are two or more letter combinations joined in one body. This is done to improve the appearance of some letter combinations, such as:

fi → fi
ffl → ffl
ct → ct

Today, there are only a few fonts that include a wide range of ligatures.

Horizontal scale refers to the horizontal width of letters which can be scaled in desktop typography to distort the original form of any font.

It's best to use this tool sparingly.

SCALE 80%
SCALE 100%
SCALE 140%

TYPE SPACING TERMINOLOGY

Kerning refers to the subtracting of space between letters, especially letters set in all caps and at large sizes. It is done to improve the aesthetic look and balance of the letter combinations, especially in large type on bookcovers. It is often overlooked on poorly typeset covers.

WORK ⎰ The word "Work" without extra *kerning*. When set large, the spacing looks uneven, especially between the "w" and "o."

WORK ⎰ The word "work" with *kerning applied*. The spaces between the letters, "w" and "o" and "r" are reduced.

Tracking refers to the average space between letters in a line or block of text.

BOOK TITLE ← Without tracking applied

B O O K T I T L E ← With tracking applied

Leading (pronounced *ledding*) refers to the distance between the baseline of a line of text and the baseline of the line of text below it. Primary leading is the leading used in the general body text and secondary leading refers to amounts that may be used in particular instances, such as between numbered paragraphs or between paragraphs and lists.

This line of text is set in 8 point Garamond using 9 point leading. This leading is too tight, causing the letter ascenders and descender to crash together.

This line of text is set in 8 point Garamond using 10 point leading. This greater leading provides more space between the lines and is more readable.

Word spacing refers to the amount of spacing between the words in a line of text. If the space is too tight or too loose, the reader will find the text less legible and more tiring to read. Good typesetting should both make the book look interesting and provide a good experience for the user.

The word spacing in this paragraph is uniform and not too tight, making it easy to read and looks better than the uneven word spacing shown below.

The word spacing in this paragraph is uniform and not too tight, making it easy to read and look better than the uneven word spacing shown below.

> **Tip** Your contract needs to state that the files must be *press ready* or *print ready,* with the written understanding that the provider of the final files is obligated to provide you with files that the printer can actually use.

will not print because the PDF (postscript document format) file was prepared incorrectly, and this can be remedied by minor file adjustments and/or simply using different PDF settings.

Because of these complexities and the number of things that can go wrong, the best practice is to use a designer and/or production person who has experience with books. Your contract should always state that the files must be *press-ready* or *print-ready,* with the written understanding that the provider of the final files is obligated to provide you with files that the printer can actually use.

It's not unusual for the press-ready files to run into snags at the printer that require some minor tweaks and adjustments. Your designer or whoever prepared the files should be able and willing to work directly with the printer to sort out any technical difficulties. You shouldn't have to be involved or troubled by the technicalities of such incidentals.

In addition to the page files, the cover file must be laid out so that it actually fits the size of the book. The most common book formats are *hardback* and *paperback.* The cover layout includes the spine and back cover for paperbacks and additional flaps if it has a book jacket or dust cover for a hardback book. These are not, however, the only options. There are paperback books with flaps, too, called *French flaps,* as well as layouts for other types of bindings, such as *concealed wire-O binding.* There are cover layouts that are mechanically glued to the cover board, called *casewraps,* and sometimes covered by a removable jacket with the same cover design. Every option requires its own layout specifications.

The person or persons in charge of cover production must understand the size and positioning requirements necessary for creating these types of covers. In order for the cover image and title to align properly, the width of the spine has to be set in the layout according to the bulk size of the type of paper chosen and the number of pages contained in the book. The layout must account for the difference between page trim size and the actual jacket size needed to cover the hardback binding, and so on.

Tip Avoid problems by having your providers work together to check each other's work. One provider's okay on their own work isn't enough.

Steps for checking printer proofs and ensuring that the cover fits correctly are described in the Chapter 8, *Your Publishing Options: eBooks, Print on Demand, and Process Printing.*

PROOFREADING

Once all the pages are typeset and laid out, everything needs to be proofread. This includes the cover and any other files sent to the printer—that is, all files that have some text, positioning, colors, etc., must be checked.

The first set of typeset pages is called the "first pass." For the first pass, the normal procedure is for the author and editor to read and check the entire text. Any author alterations required are sent to the copy editor who will edit the changes and mark them on the first-pass page layouts, either marking actual printouts or using the tools in a program like Adobe Acrobat to mark the digital file (the PDF). The marked file is then returned to the layout artist. Only the designer/copyfitter proficient with the layout program can key-in the changes and adjust the copyfitting before creating and returning the second-pass pages to the copy editor. The editor/proofreader will check the changes and send a copy of the second pass to the author and/or publisher.

For the second pass, the normal procedure is for the author and editor to check only the changes that were made to the first pass. If they find any additional key-in errors or omissions or other needed editorial changes, these are marked on the second-pass pages and returned to the copyfitter. This process will continue back-and-forth until there are no more alterations to be made or errors found to correct. At this stage, the pages are approved and the press-ready file(s) are generated and sent to the printer who will send proofs to the author/publisher to check *before* final printing begins.

Typically, a book goes through about three or four passes. It's important to make the changes at one time or at each complete pass. That is, don't call the designer or typesetter every time you find one thing that needs changes. Instead, complete the needed proofreading of all the pages and send all requests at one time. Otherwise the designer or typesetter will have to keep locating and opening your files to make the key-ins. This wastes time. Likewise, don't send twenty e-mails with different requests. Instead, collect all the needed changes and send them at one time.

PROOFREADING PAGE LAYOUTS

Below are some basic proofreading tips and suggestions for page layouts. Different projects have different requirement. This is not a comprehensive list. Proofreading is best left to a professional, but you may want to do some basic checks of your own, such as the ones listed below, to reduce the chance that the book will go to print containing needless errors.

TEXT ACCURACY, DESIGN, AND LAYOUT CHECKS

► *Cross-reference and accuracy checks*

☐ Check the accuracy of the page numbers in the table of contents.

☐ Check that all running heads match the wording of the chapter titles/book title.

☐ Check the page numbers in any references that appear in the text.

☐ Check the heads and all other elements for correct text and consistent alignments.

☐ Check typographic elements (hyphens, en-dashes, and em-dashes for correct application, correct math symbols instead of letter substitutes, quotation marks instead of inch symbols and vice versa, etc.).

► *Design and layout checks*

☐ Check spacing before and after bulleted lists, numbered lists, extracts, etc.

☐ Check the main texts for orphans and widows.

☐ Check the main texts lines for loose or tight lines, and double spaces.

☐ Check that text in photos is not backwards.

☐ Check photos for noticeable color mode or resolution issues.

☐ View all the pages as two-page spreads to check the page tweening (text column bottom alignment is the same for both pages).

Separate out all the main style elements in the book (boxed text, quizzes, tip boxes, etc.) and compare them together for style inconsistencies. For example, separate out the chapter opener pages and place them together to spot style or alignment inconsistencies.

For reviewing printer proofs (samples of the printed book prior to final printing), see the Proofreading Printer Proofs Checklist on page 174 for additional proofreading tips and suggestions.

The growing trend for many publishers is to do the proofing and editing of the passes directly in the PDFs because this removes the costs of printouts and shipping, as well as the longer wait time involved with shipping. Everything can be done over the Internet. This process has real advantages and is likely to grow in popularity, but on average, editors/proofreaders find it easier to spot the problems on actual printouts. Nevertheless, even if the editor makes a printout, they can enter the changes into the PDF and no shipping fees or shipping delays need to occur. In some cases, the editor/proofreader may require that you cover the costs of printouts, or even make the printouts and ship them, especially if color printouts are required.

Text alterations and corrections should be expected. It is important for authors to understand that they need to be on the lookout for author and editor errors, as well as for errors by the copyfitter and printer. Instructing a typesetter to make a change doesn't mean that it will be done, or done correctly. When there are hundreds of small changes, some things get overlooked or are done incorrectly. Every change must be checked, and authors not willing to do this, or inexperienced in the process, are wise to hire a proofreader. Some errors are subtle, such as fonts that switch at the print proof stage to a wrong but similar font or disappear from the file during output. Everything must be checked—things you would reasonably expect to happen and those you would not.

Software programs are becoming more complex and are updated frequently and require continual learning and troubleshooting. Most page layout programs use master pages and master styles. Making alterations to a master style to change something in one part of the book can cause changes to other parts or styles in the book. After the last changes it is wise to check all the pages one last time before sending the files to the press.

Proofreading is an art as well as a skill, and not all proofreaders are equal in ability. A good proofreader will understand typography and page layout. They will spot loose lines, incorrect use of type characters, inconsistent applications of element styles and a wide range of issues that are often missed by authors and typesetters. If a change doesn't look like it was made, for example, a good proofreader will check carefully to see if it may have been made in the wrong line of nearby text by mistake—meaning you would have had two errors instead of one if the proofreader hadn't found it!

> **Tip** Be on the lookout for author and editor errors, as well as new errors introduced by the copy-fitter and printer. If you don't proofread, expect to feel the pain later. Your providers are not infallible, and mistakes are normal. So check all pages.

PROOFREADER MARKS

Using proofreader marks will greatly reduce the amount of typesetting errors and confusion about the changes being requested. For standard marking conventions and examples, see the Quick Guide: Typographic Characters and Quick Guide: Basic Type Terminology on pages 135–136 and Quick Guide: Type Spacing Terminology on page 137. It is possible for authors to note the changes they want without using professional proofreader marks, but if you use unconventional marks you may need to include additional explanations to avoid confusion.

KEEPING TRACK OF PROOFING COSTS

Everyone involved in the editing, typesetting, and proofreading process, except for the author, needs to be paid for their time. Publishers, not wishing to pay the costs of author alterations and printer errors, developed a system for tracking all the changes made to the typeset pages. In this system, all alterations are marked in the hardcopy margin as *AAs*, *EAs*, and *PEs*, or are color-coded or put in a Note on the pages in the PDF files.

> **Tip** Author/editor changes to the typeset page layouts are often an unanticipated, but normal cost, in publishing. The best way to reduce these costs is to have your manuscript carefully edited before typesetting.

AAs refer to *author alterations*, and the author is expected to pay for the total number of AAs. Fees per alteration vary. Typically, typesetters charge by the word, or line, or by the hour, and the author pays according to the percentage of AAs. EAs refer to *editor alterations*—meaning the alterations the editor should have caught before the manuscript was typeset. This is the cost covered by the publisher, or the author, in the case of self-publishing authors. PEs refer to *printer errors*. In the past, it was common for printers to provide the typesetting services, and make any last minute changes that were discovered in the final proofreading of page layouts. That is, PEs indicate the *key-ins* of typesetters that are, for example, misplaced or misspelled. Today, PEs may have nothing to do with the printer because many books are typeset in design studios before being sent to the printer, but they indicate errors made at the typesetting or print stages.

Author/editor changes to the typeset page layouts are often an unanticipated, but normal cost, in publishing. The best way to reduce these costs is to have your manuscript carefully edited before typesetting.

It is extremely rare for there to be no AAs, EAs, and PEs in a book project. Everyone occasionally makes mistakes. A high number of AAs and EAs will increase the number of PEs. As a self-publishing author, you are in effect the publisher, and you must therefore bear the typesetter's fees for AAs and EAs. It is tedious to keep track of who is making the mistakes and changes, and many authors and copyfitters therefore choose not to do it. Instead, the editor and copyfitter simply charge by the hour for finding and fixing the errors, respectively. Several hundred alterations may take several hours because changes may cause other copyfitting problems.

PRESS-READY FILE CREATION

It used to be that all the page files were sent to the printer, including the fonts and support documents (art linked to the pages). Font software licenses or purchase agreements now restrict the distribution of font software, and new document software has actually eliminated the need to distribute font files so it is no longer necessary. Today, most all projects are delivered to printers in the form of press-ready PDFs. PDFs can be created from many application programs including word processing programs. However, designers use page layout programs to create their designs, and the PDFs are generated from these programs instead.

The designer/copyfitter will not be using the word processing program that you used to write your book. This may change in the future, but presently designers use specialized software to create books. There have been many changes in the industry in the last decade. At present, most designers use either QuarkXPress or Adobe InDesign, but this could change in the future.

The designer/copyfitter will import the text from your document file and put it into whatever page layout program they are using. When the page layouts are complete, they will generate a PDF or series of PDFs—one for each pass until all editing and proofing is complete and the book has been approved for print. With your final approval, the designer/copyfitter will create the press-ready PDF. In some cases, printers will send the book designer or layout artist special software to install that enables him or her to create PDFs that will work better on their particular printing press. Software programs and requirements are constantly changing, and this is one of the reasons so many publishers choose to outsource their design and production. They don't want the costs involved in the software updates or training.

PREPRESS MARKETING MATERIALS

During the prepress production stage, many publishers will also have the designer start creating marketing materials. Publishers will, for example, take the designed first- or second-pass pages and have them composed into an ARC (advance reading copy). An ARC is a complete or select set of designed pages bound into a pre-publication book that will be sent to select reviewers. It will usually say on the cover that this is not the final edited version and that it is for review purposes only or something like "Advance Reading Copy—Not for Resale."

In some cases when the main editing is complete, a publisher will also have a smaller sampling of the book made, usually only the front matter plus a sample chapter bound for promotional purposes and for getting bookstores interested in the book. The smaller booklets are called *blads* and the back cover will contain a shorter version of the usual book and author information, and an outline of the planned media marketing campaign and any distributor(s) who has already agreed to carry the book. Blads are usually printed in small numbers using a print-on-demand method or as ebooks. Printed blads are too small for a spine and are therefore bound using the saddle-stitch method (staples), which means an additional cover layout is also specially prepared for this purpose.

> **Tip** Don't pass up the opportunity during prepress production to put together blads and ARCs for advanced marketing purposes.

FINAL PRESS-READY FILES

When the designer or person doing the prepress production prepares the files to go to the printer, there will be a final set of checks to ensure the files are complete and correctly prepared before delivery to the printer. Bear this in mind if you're self-publishing and you have just given the design

> **Tip** As a final precaution to prevent needless extra print proofs, have the designer send you a copy of both the final press-ready file and the documentation. Check these for any unintended alterations such as shifts in the text or fonts that don't appear correctly, before giving the okay to deliver the files to the printer.

studio your approval to send the files to the printer. It will go to the printer quickly, but first there is a final set of checks conducted by the designer or layout artist. These involve checking the fonts to ensure they are the correct format and are embedded in the file. In some cases, if it hasn't already been done, it will also mean checking to make sure all the art is saved in the correct format and resolution. The production person will prepare some documentation for the printer that includes file specifications and possibly the fonts used (even though the fonts will not be sent, some printers still request this information). As a final precaution, have the designer send you a copy of both the final press-ready files sent to the printer and the documentation. Check these for any unintended alterations such as shifts in the text or fonts that don't appear correctly.

ARCHIVING

The final files should be archived, both the press-ready PDFs and the software application files used to create them, along with any support documents. As mentioned earlier, most font license agreements do not allow designers to distribute copies of the fonts to other parties, even for the purpose of archiving them. Instead, the designer will furnish a list of the fonts and the font foundries that sell them. The design studio that has the fonts can make any future changes to the book, or the fonts can be purchased for a different studio. Some fonts with the same names are created by different foundries or exist in different versions and if substituted can cause the text to shift, leading to a wide range of serious page layout problems that can be time-consuming to fix, so it is important, if possible, to acquire the exact fonts.

One must, however, accept that no matter what precautions are taken, in some cases old digital files can become nearly impossible to open or recover. Some are improperly backed up, some saved on media that is no longer readable, others created in programs or versions of programs that are no longer in use. The most common problem is that the original files were created using a page layout program in an improper manner making new revisions too difficult to implement. In such cases, it may be necessary to extract or retype the text and recreate new page files. It may also be that the book is so out of date or poorly designed that it needs an entirely new design anyway. In any case, you still want to archive the final version of the book and all the files that went into creating it.

Your Publishing Options:
eBooks, Print on Demand, and
Process Printing

Today authors and publishers can choose between three basic forms of book duplication.

- ebooks (both PDFs and digital books for e-reading devices)
- print-on-demand (POD)
- traditional process printing

Which method or methods you choose depends on a number of factors such as your marketing strategy, audience, and finances. You will have to evaluate your options carefully to make the right decision. I recommend that authors understand all three options because there are good reasons to use them all. It is not simply a matter of one or the other, but how to use all three options together or at different times to achieve different goals. Let's start by looking at the benefits offered with ebooks.

EBOOKS

eBooks are digital files. This publication method provides an affordable and efficient opportunity to distribute books online. The books don't have to be printed because they can be read on computers. It's likely that ebooks, more than print-on-demand (POD), represent the future of publishing. ebooks are paperless books that offer both an alternative and a complement to traditional print publishing.

The economic advantages of ebooks are particularly noticeable. Printing is the largest single upfront publishing cost for most books. If you use ebooks as an alternative to print, that cost can be eliminated. If the book is distributed through your own business Web site, there are no distributor fees or warehouse storage costs.

Even if you eliminate the much larger costs of process printing thousands of books at one time by using print-on-demand (POD), ebooks still have the economic advantage over POD. Let's say that you print your 160-page color book using print-on-demand technology for the unit cost of $22.00 per book. A distributor wants 50–55%, meaning you would have to price the book at about $45 to retain a small profit. So, to avoid the distributor cut, you sell it yourself for $28.00 per copy. This gives you only a $6.00 profit per book, minus other expenses. As an alternative, you could publish and sell the same color book as an ebook for as little as $6.00 and do just as well.

eBook publishing can be used to support print publishing, too. It is an excellent marketing tool. An author can, for example, publish a book first online as an ebook in serial form and even allow readers to participate interactively with aspects of the contents. In some cases, authors have pub-

QUICK GUIDE	EBOOK ADVANTAGES

ADVANTAGES FOR PUBLISHERS

eBooks offer strong advantages to publishers over print publications, such as:

- Faster availability and easier distribution to a world-wide market.
- Content security—such as access and/or print encryption security.
- Limited or perpetual availability.
- Elimination of paper and print costs.
- Elimination of physical warehouse and archival storage requirements.
- Reduced limitations on page count.
- Dramatically reduced environmental impact.

ADVANTAGES FOR READERS

The reader or consumer, likewise receives many benefits, such as:

- Instant and perpetual availability through the Internet.
- Increased portability and easy storage.
- Internal hyperlinks for cross-referencing and access to the Web.
- Backlighting for reading in dark or low-light environments.
- Readability without having to hold a book.
- Text-to-audio reading.

lished books for a limited time as ebooks, in part or complete, for free, and people have still bought the printed book. ebooks offer advantages to both publishers and readers (see the Quick Guide: eBook Advantages above).

eBooks are ideal for academic and technical books that are in fields with extremely limited readership. They are useful for publications of long reports and reference books with limited marketability or anything too expensive to print.

Training manuals, merchandise catalogs, and other information resources that customers find useful or interesting, but might not be willing to buy, are another good use for ebooks. Books that cannot justify the costs of printing can still be published, but as ebooks.

Most books, however, will have a lower perceived value when published as ebooks. This may mean selling at a lower cover price. People still prefer to read a book they can hold in their hands. Unless printing on paper and transporting books becomes so expensive that it is prohibitive, it is unlikely that ebooks will ever replace printed books. Nevertheless, ebook demand is increasing every year and very substantially. Even if publishers continue to print books, the volume of ebooks published will likely overtake printed books in the near future.

THE EBOOK DESIGN ADVANTAGE

Presently, ebooks may have a lower perceived value in general, but this is not true of all ebooks. Some ebooks offering business secrets and valuable information are actually sold at prices far in excess of most trade books. eBooks can also be designed so that the perceived value is high without increasing other production costs, since there is no printing required.

eBooks can look exactly like traditional books and can, in fact, with minor adjustments, be generated from the same files that are used to generate press-ready files for process printing and print-on-demand. Because ebooks can be designed as nicely as any printed book, there is no necessary loss in design quality or typesetting standards. Some consumers even prefer ebooks to printed books because they can be stored and read on portable laptops.

When an ebook is not generated from files made for a process printed book, the ebook designer can create a book that is free from the cost restraints of color printing. ebooks only require low-resolution images and that reduces the costs of using stock photography. This allows publishers to create ebooks economically with value-added content and design features. Using design to enhance a publisher's or a business's brand identity becomes much more economical with ebooks.

eBook challenges

Despite all the advantages of e-books, there are some challenges that publishers need to know about. Currently, one of these challenges involves font licenses. Most font software restricts e-book usage unless an additional royalty is paid. Some font providers require annual payments. There are, however, a few providers that do not restrict e-book usage, and Adobe licenses many fonts that can be embedded in PDFs.

This common font software restriction is largely unknown to publishers and designers, but legal disputes suggest that this issue will get more attention in the years ahead. The problem is that font software embedded inside PDFs (the e-book) can be illegally extracted by other users (readers). To safeguard their intellectual property, font providers place license restrictions on e-books. You have to decide whether the extra costs are justified or whether your need to instruct your designer to locate unrestricted fonts that are suitable for your project. Always check your font licenses before creating and distributing e-books.

Publishers may also be concerned about e-book piracy. The vast majority of e-books available today are distributed as PDFs, and these can include a variety of security features

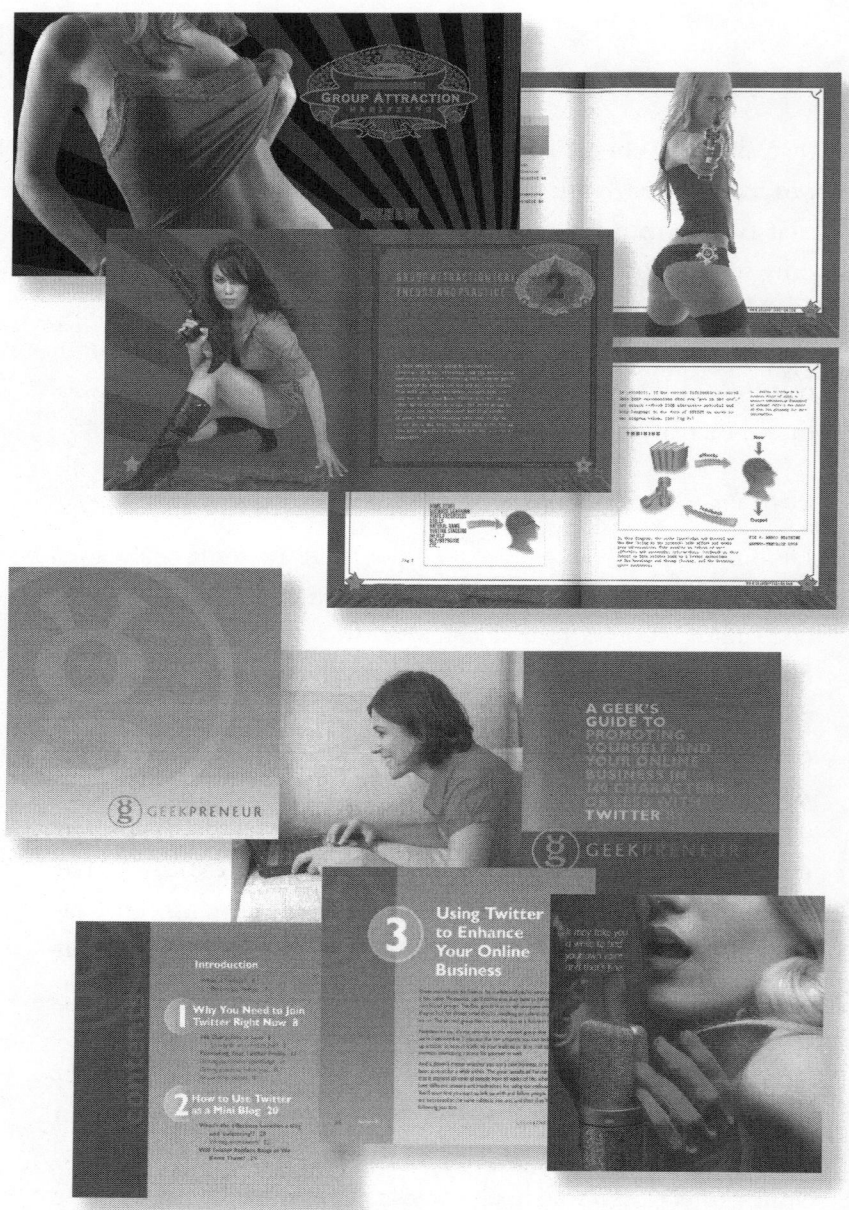

Some book format sizes, such as 8.5"x8.5", are more easily adaptable to different publication methods. With advanced planning, I was able to design and set up the files for the two books above, *Group Attraction* (top) and *A Geek's Guide* (bottom) so that they could, with minor file adjustments, have the option to be published as ebooks, print-on-demand books, and traditional process printed books.

that prevent alteration, text extraction, and/or printing. The truth is that piracy is a problem for all forms of publication.

PDFs are, by far, the most universally used format for creating great looking e-books with the widest audience reach, but there are other alternatives. A number of companies have launched portable e-book readers, such as Amazon's Kindle, Sony's Reader Digital Book, Tianjin Jinke Electronics' Hanlin eReader, iRex's iLiad, and so on. Most e-readers are black-and-white only, and best-suited for books that are text only with no value-added formatting such as navigation graphics or color diagrams. It is likely that e-reader technology will improve quickly in the years ahead. Nevertheless, rather than an alternative publishing format, these devices represent an additional channel of distribution. More will be said about e-book readers in *Book Marketing Essentials*.

Tip Make sure you understand your font license agreement before publishing ebooks because some do not allow font embedding or require additional royalties for ebooks.

PRINT-ON-DEMAND

Print-on-demand (POD) offers an additional publishing option or alternative to traditional process printing. In fact, POD offers some very attractive advantages over process printing (see Quick Guide: Print-on-Demand Pros and Cons, on page 159). You can print only the copies you need as they are ordered. If you need more copies for a special event, you can get copies more quickly, especially when compared to process printing in a foreign country. You don't have to warehouse large numbers of books or pay for storage. You can revise the book more often without the problem of unsold earlier editions.

There are however, some serious downsides to print-on-demand. The most noticeable problem is the high unit costs and the lower print quality. The unit costs are much higher, so you will make less profit per book sold—especially for color books—unless you sell the books directly and cut out other distributors. In some cases you may have to give up color altogether. Distributors want 50% or more of the cover price. Your profit is from what remains after you deduct your other production and marketing expenses. This means you would have to price the book too high to compete with process-printed books. This makes the book so unlikely to sell that distributors will not carry it.

The high unit costs of POD makes this option more ideal for very specialized book projects that can be priced high or for books that are only required in a small quantity. Apart from such unique situations, POD is best for people who don't care if they make any profit from their books. In this case, POD is best for books that are intended for a small audience, such as one's own family and friends—books such as scrapbooks, photo albums, family letters, special event publications, etc.

The quality of POD is continually improving, and it is possible that some day all *printed* books will use this method. But currently, the quality is not there. The lower quality is not only the color or black-and-white images, but the actual ink permanence, color lightfastness, and print consistency. POD publishing is basically photocopying. Likewise, the

... ...

QUICK GUIDE	PRINT-ON-DEMAND PROS AND CONS

ADVANTAGES

Like ebook publishing, print-on-demand offers important advantages over traditional process book printing, including:

- Little up-front investment is required.
- Quick delivery.
- There are no large quantities of books to store in your garage.
- Revisions to the book are less problematic.
- Better for the environment. No paper used.

DISADVANTAGES

Disadvantages of POD publishing that limit the usefulness of this option include:

- Higher unit costs (which rules out distribution through most all book stores)
- Print quality is lower and less consistent.
- There are fewer trim size, paper choice, and binding options.
- There is no large ready inventory of books to sell.
- Books have a recognizably lower perceived value for consumers.

accuracy of page trim and alignments is often extremely irregular—sometimes off by as much as nearly half an inch! Binding options are limited, and paper options usually consist of nothing more than one type of white or cream.

Some POD printers have lower standards than others, and it is wise to ask around if you are unfamiliar with a printer. A POD book may at first look like a typical book, but the binding may fail before you can finish reading it. Other POD limitations include things like how many pages a color book can have. Some POD printers, for example, will only print full-color books that are no longer than 100 or 250 pages. Different suppliers offer a wider range of options, but at the present time authors who require fewer limitations and higher quality need to use the process method.

> **Tip** If you plan to rely on book-shops for distribution, the high unit costs of POD will likely present an insurmount-able obstacle for bookstores to carry your book.

BEST USES OF POD

If you take care to invest a year or more in writing a book with real market potential, you may not want to go cheap with the print-ing, especially if you have invested in quality editing and design. Even so, POD can be useful. It is certainly the best way to produce advance review copies for marketing purposes. It is a good way to test a book's utility and appeal before investing in process printing. It can also be used to keep books in print once an inventory of process printed copies has sold, but before sufficient demand has built up to justify process printing larger quantities of books again.

POD PRINTING VS. POD PUBLISHING SERVICES

Anyone interesting in POD will soon discover that there are numerous companies marketing to self-publishing authors and offering both POD print services alongside what is basically subsidy publishing or vanity publishing. It is best to make a clear distinction between POD printing and POD subsidy publishing. At present, print-on-demand publishing services are mostly a low-quality way to create a book that will go nowhere, as explained earlier in Chapter 2, *What You Must Know about Self-Publishing*. That said, it is possible to use the POD print services of many of these same companies without using their editing, design, page composition, or marketing services.

Don't be fooled by extravagant marketing claims. The truth is that none of these companies will likely get your POD book into any bookstores. A few of these companies can, however, give you a presence for your book on their Web site. Createspace, for example, is owned by Amazon and this makes getting a presence on Amazon.com easy.

> Tip   Print-on-demand provides an affordable way to put together blads and ARCs for advanced marketing purposes.

If you decide to sign up for POD as your main publishing method or for short-run promotional purposes, take care to read the fine print. Many POD providers offering "self-publishing" services are actually set up to act as publishers, and you might be signing away rights that you want to keep along with needlessly large amounts of money. The full costs can be hidden, and you may not be able to take the designed book files to a different printer if you decide to at a later date.

When it comes to POD printer contracts, I recommend Mark Levine's book, *The Fine Print of Self-Publishing: The Contracts & Services of 45 Self-Publishing Companies—Analyzed, Ranked & Exposed*. This book rates the contracts of the best-known POD providers online—the good, the bad, and the extremely ugly. He doesn't rate Lightning Source (an Ingram company), because they are serving publishers, and he is interested in ones that are marketing services to self-publishing authors. (Comments on Levine's book refer to the 3rd edition.) More on POD and marketing will be explained in *Book Marketing Essentials*.

PROCESS PRINTING

If you want your book to be sold through bookstores, or to be in a unique format, or to be a high-quality print product, then you must use process printing. As I will explain, it is extremely unlikely that a POD book will make it into bookshops.

Process printing requires the highest upfront financial investment, but gives the publisher the lowest unit cost and the highest print quality. The unit cost is the cost required to print each book. That is, it requires a large upfront investment to print large quantities of books, but the higher the quantity, the lower the costs of producing each book, and that means the publisher can profit more from each sale. The low unit cost is one of the keys to getting into bookshops, even more than quality printing. Process printing is the dominant method used—in fact, nearly the only method used—for books carried by bookshops.

The two main drawbacks to process printing are:

1 **Initial costs:** It requires more money upfront. Also, if you discover something wrong in the book, you may still need to sell a percentage of the books to make back the printing costs and capture a profit before considering printing new editions to correct the error. Process printing requires

QUICK GUIDE PROCESS PRINTING PROS AND CONS

The advantages and disadvantages of process printing are the opposite of print-on-demand.

ADVANTAGES

The advantages of process printing:

- The unit costs is low. This makes competitive pricing possible and that increases the likelihood of distribution through most book stores.
- It can provide the highest and most consistent print quality.
- It offers the widest range of format options (numerous trim sizes, paper choices, binding options, etc.). This means you have a greater opportunity to differentiate your book product from the competition.
- It enables you to have a large ready inventory of books to sell.
- It offers a higher perceived value to the consumer.

DISADVANTAGES

Process printing disadvantages include:

- It requires a high up-front investment.
- It involves a slow initial delivery.
- It requires that you find storage space for a large quantities of books.
- Revisions to the book are difficult because of reprinting costs.

commitment, especially when ordering very large quantities. This cost is one of the main reasons publishers established such strict standards and procedures for quality control.

2 **Storage:** Once you print 10,000 or more books, you will probably need to pay to warehouse them somewhere. Even though there are "fulfillment" businesses that specialize in book storage and distributions, it is an added cost. If you have only one or two books and only print 1,000 or 3,000

copies each, the usual minimums for process printing, you may be able to store them at home.

Many authors imagine that their books will be sold in the millions and assume the publisher will want to print a huge quantity. The reality is that most books are printed in small quantities or short print runs—usually 2,000–8,000 copies, sometimes many fewer if it's an academic book. Large publishers may start off some titles in larger numbers, such as 10,000 and above. But only the established best-selling authors, the superstars, or books with extremely hot titles get six- and seven-figure print runs. It is more likely that a successful book will be printed in small quantities many times. Most niche books sell best in their first year, with sales declining gradually every year after, meaning that additional print runs, if any, will be smaller, rather than larger. But be aware that some printers will not offer any price difference on print runs under 3,000 copies. That is, they will print 1,000 or 2,000 as requested, but the total print run price may not be much less than if they were being asked to print 3,000 copies.

It is because most books are printed and sold in such small quantities that only the publisher can hope to gain a worthwhile profit from the book—and because more and more authors are discovering this, they are choosing to self-publish. When books are sold in small quantities, the only way authors can make much money is by publishing and selling the books themselves.

Even though process printing costs are a relatively large upfront investment, for most books, even color books, this entire cost can usually be recovered before the first thousand books are sold. This means self-publishing authors who sell

Process printing offers many benefits and possibilities that are presently unavailable with the print-on-demand option. For this women's healthcare guide, the client wanted a unique high-quality product that could be produced affordably in large quantities. The cover is printed on the inside as well as on the front and back. The spiral binding is a concealed wire-O binding, meaning that the cover folds around it to conceal the binding. The book includes custom die-cut tabs printed on a heavier paper and a pocket on the back for inserts. These features, along with embossing, foils, and varnishes, are only available and cost-effective using the traditional process method.

their own books can make an attractive profit from even a short print run of 3,000 books.

Process printing options in the global marketplace

In the late 20th-century, Asian printing companies worked hard to gain the lead in process color printing. They established offices in countries throughout the world, and today many of the best-quality color books are printed in Asia. Some complicated types of projects, such as those involving certain types of die cuts, are often more easily done in Asia than in America or Europe. At present, the trend to outsource printing to Asia continues, and even U.S. printers are getting in on the practice.

Even though the costs are higher—sometimes 2–3 times higher—U.S. publishers still get good deals from U.S. printers for substantial quantities of color books. But overall, from a cost point of view, smaller publishers may find it preferable to print black-and-white books in the U.S. or Europe and color books in Asia.

Getting reduced prices by working with printers in Asia requires additional shipping time, which is usually about 5–6 weeks. The complete project time required is, on average, 2–4 months, from delivery of press-ready files to receipt of finished books. The schedule might look something like this:

> File delivered to Hong Kong office: February 1
> Proofs express from Hong Kong: February 22
>   (include Chinese New Year holiday)
> Marked proofs returned to Hong Kong: March 3
> Revise proofs and imposed ozalids express from Hong Kong:
>   March 17

Ozalids approval communicated to Hong Kong: March 25
Actual printing: April 2
Books shipped from Hong Kong: April 30.

RTS (Ready to ship) dates might be on Wednesdays and sailing dates the following Monday. Books sent from Hong Kong all the way to the State of Maine (U.S.), can arrive at the door in five weeks. This example is taken from an actual project.

On the printer's estimate, you may see a notice that says, "client responsible for paying duty tax." This is there for non-book products. At the present time, there are no duty taxes on books shipped to the USA.

Selecting a process printer

When selecting a printer—even printers recommended by a designer—always ask for references and for printed book examples. Describe your project to the printer, and they will likely send you something similar to demonstrate their abilities. Have a contract, and request a schedule.

Paper choices

There is a huge variety of paper choices available for process printing. The cost-effective approach is to use a choice already stocked by the printer. You may want to pick a paper simply based on how it looks in a book you've seen. Ask your designer before you commit. The paper used will affect the printing.

For text stock, most papers fall into two categories: coated and uncoated: Coated papers are either matte, semi-gloss, or gloss, and sometimes high-gloss. Coated papers absorb less ink and produce brighter colors. These papers are best for picture books, such as photo books and children's books. Light reflections on gloss papers can be irritating to readers, so matte or semi-gloss is often a better choice for how-to books.

Uncoated papers are what you'll find in most novels. These papers are more absorbent and are best for books that are all text. If you ever look at a Pantone color matching system, they show colors in two categories, coated and uncoated. This will help give you an idea of how the same colors will appear on coated and uncoated papers.

All papers come in weights, or different thicknesses. Text weight is specified in grams or pounds, but because weights are determined by sheet size, the system can be confusing. An 80 lb. cover stock is thicker than an 80 lb. text stock. For this reason, you should request samples.

Make sure you receive paper samples *with the specifications written on them*. Printers sometimes substitute cheaper paper to save money, so you must have a contract that specifies the paper type and a sample provided by the printer that matches the contract. The specifications for the paper must be written on the paper sample by the printer and include any information about the paper stated in the contract, such as finish (matte, semi-gloss, gloss, high-gloss) and weight. If this is omitted, then you must request new paper samples that match what is stated in the contract! This must be done before the wet proofs are made or any printing takes place.

Special printing options

Process printers can offer many specialized services beyond regular color printing. You can, for example, request spot varnishes, metallic inks, die cuts, foldouts, pockets for

✓ PROCESS PRINTER ESTIMATES

In addition to the contract with its usual clauses on terms of payment, confidentiality, liability, conflict resolution, etc., make sure your estimate includes specific project details and specifications, such as:

- ☐ Book title
- ☐ Type of binding (hardcover, softcover, spiral, etc.)
- ☐ Proposed quantities with the unit price (individual book price they are charging—i.e., not your price on the book—and the final total costs for the full quantity)
- ☐ Types and costs of proofs to be provided
- ☐ Trim size
- ☐ Page count
- ☐ Materials used: paper choice (weight and finish, such as 128 gsm glossy artpaper) for each aspect of the book project, such as interior pages, endpapers, cover jacket, etc.
- ☐ Orientation (portrait or landscape)
- ☐ Packing method of final books (e.g., kraftwrapped in cartons on pallets)
- ☐ Shipping costs with point of origin and final delivery destination
- ☐ Any costs for additional features and printing, such as embossing or gold foil

Any needed specification may vary depending on your project requirements. Make sure that the printer supplies you with a sample of the paper stipulated in the contract with a note confirming the correlation. Ideally, the paper sample should have the specification written on it. This is critically important because printers may intentionally or unintentionally substitute your choice of paper for a cheaper or less desirable option when the book is printed.

inserts, etc. These features can help you differentiate your book from your competition.

In color printing, the full range of colors is created through a process of small dots that use only four colors—cyan (C), magenta (M), yellow (Y), and black (represented by the letter K)—known as *4-color* or *CMYK* process printing. If you see an estimate that says "4/1" this simply means full color on one side and one color (usually black) on the other side. The shorthand "4/4" means full color both sides.

Many color presses are 4-color presses, but many large printing presses today often include the capability of 1 or 2 more additional spot inks so that when the paper goes through the press, exact spot colors (including metallic inks, or laminates and/or varnishes) can be added at the same time. It is often worthwhile to talk with your designer about the possibility of improving the look of your book with these features. An experienced designer will be able to make recommendations for your book and create the necessary files for the printer.

Proofing methods, samples, and printer templates

Process printers will provide several types of proofs depending on the book project. For black-and-white books, you will receive *ozalids*. Ozalids are monocolor proofs (also known as blue lines, diazo, etc.). For black-and-white books, this form of inexpensive proof is sufficient. For color books, additional color proofs are required. With ozalid proofs, all text or color content (for color books) are represented in one color, which is blue, black, or brown. Ozalids are not printed on the paper used in the actual printing of the book. Process-printed books are composed of signatures (usually a division consisting of 16 pages), and ozalids are, therefore, supplied in loose equivalent signatures. The ozalid pages are printed on both sides and are like an unbound book. Use ozalids to check accurate text positioning on the page and correct pagination (order of pages). If you've ever seen blue architectural plans, you may already be familiar with the ozalid method.

For color books, you will likely receive ozalids and either *wet proofs* and/or *digital proofs*. Wet proofs are the best method and are printed pages using the actual ink and paper that will be used for your final book. Wet proofs are the most reliable proofing method, but also the most expensive. If a problem involving color is found, then the file must be corrected or printing adjusted, and then new wet proofs are required to show that the correction has been made. The final printed book should match the quality of the *approved* wet proof. Wet proofs may be supplied in the form of large sheets or stacks of one-sided pages with trim marks and margin color bars.

> Tip   Don't tempt the printer. The paper specifications must be written on the paper sample by the printer and match the specifications in the contract.

Digital proofs are basically photocopies or inkjet printouts and are therefore much less accurate. Each method has its purpose. If you make a type or placement correction (rather than a color correction) after seeing wet proofs, you don't need the expense of new wet proofs. Instead, you can request a digital proof, or even a PDF, that will show you that the correction has been made.

When you receive your proofs, check them for uneven printing, undesirable color tints, and artifacts such as spots, file corruption, pagination errors, misalignments, etc. Write any desired changes or corrections directly on the proofs as

PROOFREADING PRINTER PROOFS

In addition to rechecking any of the matters listed in the Proofreading Manuscripts Checklist on page 91 and the Proofreading Page Layouts Checklist on page 141, use the basic list below as a guide for checking printer proofs. It is best to have a qualified designer check the proofs for you and act as your mediator to fix any issues that you want changed or corrected on the proofs.

► *Checking ozalids (for all types of books)*

☐ Are all the pages included?

☐ Are pages in the correct order?

☐ Are page numbers correct?

☐ Are all the photos displaying in the correct position?

☐ Are all the fonts displaying correctly?

☐ Does the text look clear, even, and shark?

☐ Do bleeds extend beyond trim marks?

☐ Is the trim size accurate?

► *Checking wet proofs (for color process books) and digital proofs (for color process and POD books)*

☐ Are all the pages included?

☐ Are the wet proofs printed on the correct paper finish and weight?

☐ Are all the photos displaying in the correct position?

☐ Are all the fonts displaying correctly?

☐ Does the text look clear, even, and sharp?

☐ Do bleeds extend beyond the trim or trim marks?

☐ Is the trim size accurate?

☐ Is the text on colored backgrounds easy to read (for example, white type on black backgrounds)?

☐ Are black areas (backgrounds) set to black or *rich black*?

For more detailed information about ozalids, wet proofs, and checking printer proofs, please read the explanations in this chapter.

well as in a letter or e-mail. Return these to the printer with the condition that new proofs must be sent showing the corrections, or, if the schedule doesn't permit that, that approval is granted only on the condition that the corrections are made.

Some forms of color correction can be made solely by the printer, and in other cases the designer or person who prepared the press-ready PDF may have to change the file and supply a new PDF. Don't expect your designer to pay for any extra proofs for changes that are requested after approved PDFs are sent to the printer.

The process of checking the proofs usually takes several hours or fewer, and your designer will often include time for this in the general estimate or offer the service for a separate fee. Getting the designer involved in the proofing is a good idea. In the past, proofing or "press checks" was almost always done on location, that is, the client and designer would go to the printer and examine samples as they rolled off the press before giving the okay to carry on with the printing. This efficient, but stressful arrangement is unnecessary and in many cases no longer encouraged by printers. I had one client fly all the way to China for a press check—which I discouraged—only for him to discover that the printer wouldn't take him to the actual printing location. Fortunately, times have changed, and most printers ship wet proofs to the client and the client can more thoroughly examine them at his or her leisure. An additional copy of the proofs can be sent to the designer who may reside in a different part of the country. Geography is no longer a barrier to getting the talent you want.

Today, fewer designers do press checks on location, especially because many projects are sent to them by out-of-state clients, and many color and complicated jobs are sent over-seas. Proofs can be sent anywhere in the world, reviewed, marked, and returned. On one project, we were unsure if the printer understood how we wanted a foldout map to be placed in the front of a book. They e-mailed four photos numbered 1–4, showing a mock up of the front matter pages being opened one by one, and the map unfolding. It was perfectly clear, and we could give the okay with confidence.

Printers will also supply a *dummy* book. This is a com-pletely blank book that is the exact size, paper choice, and binding type that will be used for your book. Use it to check those specs. It is especially important to use this to check the fit of the jacket proof.

Along with the dummy book, some printers will send a headband and/or cloth catalog or samples. These samples demonstrate your options for hardcover books. This assumes the book does not use a casewrap, which is when the printed cover is printed on paper and glued to the case board rather than covered in cloth and wrapped with a book jacket. Very narrow hardcover books, such as typical 32-page children's books are too thin to require a *headband*. The headband is the small colored cloth trim that appears at the top and bottom of the spine.

In addition to blank dummy books, printers will some-times create a handmade mock up. For one client I designed a health book with custom tabs and concealed wire-O bind-ing. The printer sent an exact fully bound mock up with hand-cut tabs.

Most printers will provide the designer with templates for the cover or jacket that have the spine width (calculated based on paper choice). In a few cases, the printer will decline and insist that they will make any necessary adjustments. And, in some cases, this is feasible, but not always. An experienced designer will want the template specs, and, if not received, to know whether or not the printer can adjust the files as required.

Refer to the Proofreading Printer Proofs Checklist on page 172 for additional tips for checking printer proofs.

THREE-WAY PUBLISHING

If you want to publish the same book files with minimum alteration in multiple ways—as an e-book, a print-on-demand book, and a quality process printed book—then there are a few simple steps you can follow to make this easier.

Have the designer determine a format size based on the sizes offered by the POD supplier you are most likely to use. POD has the most format size restrictions. Because of these limitations, you can go from POD to process printing or e-book much easier than the other way around.

If you want to do an e-book, use a POD size orientation that will open to fill the optimum viewing area of a Web page. This is about 9.5" × 13", meaning that the standard 6"× 9" book size is a good option. Most computer monitors are landscape, and this orientation provides the best user experience for viewing a full two-page spread.

Make sure all the art you provide your designer is high-resolution (300 ppi) for print. Lower-resolution files can be generated from these for e-book use.

The designer should check the POD production specs carefully before starting the design or book production. Many providers have different setup requirements. Lightning Source, for example requires that the bleed area fall within the actual page setup of the PDF file (within the normal crop mark area). This means a color book that will print POD at 8.5" × 8.5" needs to be set up in a file that will actually be 8.75" (width) × 9" (height). To use the same file in process printing, it is best to print it at 8.75" × 9" and simply add extra bleed—meaning art that bleeds needs to be 9" × 9.25". When using Lightning Source for a POD size of 8.5" × 8.5", the e-book and process printed book is slightly larger. With some other providers, the size remains the same.

The main idea is that you can have it all. You can have files created that allow for ebook publishing, print on demand, and process printing. This means you can benefits from the unique advantages of each publishing method with little extra costs is you plan in advance.

Conclusion

When you self-publish, you are becoming a real publisher even if for only one book. And, like other publishers, your tasks involve finding and project managing the professionals you need. But, as I have explained, if you work with professionals experienced in book production, the difficulty of project management can often be streamlined. Find an editor who can both edit your manuscript and proofread page layouts for typographical and design issues. And find a designer or design studio that can both design books and do page layout. Once you locate one book professional, whether an experienced editor or designer, he or she can usually connect you with any other required professional, including a printer. Always check references and portfolios, use signed agreements, and pay as you go. If you follow these practices, you should be able to create the products you want and get the positive reviews you need.

Hire your editor and designer with a view to getting them to add value to your book product. Professionals will know how to do this. You can reduce your financial risks by starting out with ebooks or print on demand. These options allow you to test your product, evaluate interest, and get reviews in advance of doing more expensive print runs.

In the previous chapters, everything you must know about self-publishing has been explained so that you can get the best results and avoid the most common errors. If this could be summarized in one key idea, it would be "Self-publish without doing all the work yourself." By this, I mean that if you want to be successful at self-publishing, follow the example of the most successful publishers by using their methods and their contractors. It starts with creating your own publisher identity with your own publisher ISBN. Then be sure to write the best book you can and hire the best book professionals to put it together for you. Let others with the know-how and experience do the hard work of producing your book for you. With this approach you can self-publish the easy way and get the results you want for your book.

Glossary

AAs. Author alterations to typeset pages.

advance (book) marketing. Marketing done in advance of publication.

ARC (advance review copy). Usually a bound copy of the printed book using print-on-demand or photocopy technology.

back matter (also called *end matter*). Last portions of a book, such as appendices, glossary, and index.

blad. Book cover and select portions of a book used for marketing purposes.

bleed. Extra image area or color area that extends beyond the edge of the page.

blue line. See *ozalid*.

buy-out. Usage fee that allows for different and unlimited uses, but doesn't require that the photographer, writer, or illustrator give up the copyright.

casewrap. Printed cover pasted to a hardback or hardcase book.

cast off. Estimated *page count*. The calculated number of pages that a manuscript will fill determined from font size, leading, and page layout design.

CMYK. Color mode setting for print and abbreviation for the four process ink colors (cyan, magenta, yellow, and black) used to create other colors in process printing.

copy editor. A copy editor or *line editor* is responsible for editing and checking the spelling, grammar, style, and punctuation of the author manuscript and any changes to typeset page layouts. Copyediting is distinct from *developmental editing*.

copyfitting. The process of adjusting type to make it fit an intended space or number of pages and of eliminating undesirable traits such as tight or loss lines. Also called *page compositing*.

crop. To cut the visible area of an image to improve its appearance.

design brief. Art direction and instructions given to a designer to help guide the design process.

developmental editor. An editor who helps the author/publisher organize and improve the content of a book.

diazo. See *ozalid.*

digital printing. Any form of desktop printing, such as laser or inkjet printing used for creating proofs for a book.

dpi (dots per inch). See also *ppi.*

domain name. A unique case-insensitive name that identifies a site on the Internet.

dummy. A handcrafted representation of a book. Some dummies are in the form of a blank book, but can include content, although that is usually called a *mock up.*

EAs. Editor alterations to the typeset book.

ebook (short for *electronic book*). Digital books read on computers or on dedicated e-reading devices.

e-reader. Device for reading ebooks.

endsheets (also called *endpapers*). Folded sheets of paper (often colored or featuring printed graphics or images) that hold the pages to the cover of hardback books—i.e., are glued to the first and last book signature and then adhered to the cover.

errata. Corrections to a book issued after publication and sometimes printed on a piece of paper and adhered to printed copies of the book.

first-pass pages. First set of complete book pages from the typesetter and page compositor. When the book pages are made ready, a *pass* is created to be proofread. A book may go through many passes.

flap. That portion of the cover on paperbacks and/or hardback books that folds inside and is concealed when the book cover is closed.

French flaps. A paperback book with cover *flaps.*

front matter. First portions of a book, such as half-title page, title page, copyright page, contents pages, preface, dedication, and acknowledgment. Usually numbered with Roman numerals so that revisions and additions to the front matter page count can be renumbered without changing the Arabic numerals of the main book, which preserves the indexing numbers and any other cross-referencing in the main text.

ghost writer. A professional writer who will write or complete a book that will officially be credited to someone else. Ghost writers usually remain anonymous.

hardcopy. A printout of the author manuscript and/or the designed page layouts.

headband. The decorative cloth element found on the head (top) and tail (bottom) of a text block spine of a bound book.

high concept. Original and unique idea in a manuscript that gives it obvious appeal. Similar to unique selling proposition (USP).

hosting. The business of providing storage and connectivity for Web sites so that they can become available on the Internet.

house style. A set of style guidelines developed by and/or adopted by a publishing house for editors and authors.

inkjet printing. A common form of relatively inexpensive desktop printing used to create color proofs of book covers and pages for inexact color proofing purposes.

interior design. When referring to books, the design of the pages inside a book.

ISBN (International Standard Book Number). A unique numerical identification for publishers and each of their books.

jacket (also called *dust jacket* or *dust cover*). Sheet of paper with a book cover image that folds around either a paperback or more commonly a hardback book.

JPEG. Digital image format often used for the Web and ebooks. Stands for *Joint Photographic Experts Group* who created the standard.

kerning. Adjusting space between letter forms so that the blank spaces are proportional.

key-in. Correction or change made to a page layout by a typesetter. Also, the process of creating a digital text file from printed or handwritten text.

LCCN (Library of Congress Control Number). A number issued by the U.S. Library of Congress that makes it easier for libraries and book dealers to access the book's bibliographic record and better process orders.

Leading (pronounced *ledding*). Height of one line of text counting the spacing between it and the next line of text.

layout. See *page layout*.

line editor. See *copy editor*.

logo. Logotype, but now applied broadly to company trademarks.

mock up. A handcrafted representation of a book or product using printouts. The purpose of a mock up is to show how the finished product will look prior to actual manufacturing, and it is also used for photographing and for advance marketing.

NDA. Non-disclosure agreement intended to protect intellectual property and proprietary information.

orphan. First line of a paragraph at the bottom of a page. An undesirable copyfitting error to be avoided.

ozalid. A monocolor printing method used to create page proofs for checking text, pagination, and page elements.

page count. The total number of pages in a section of a book or in a complete book.

page layout. The design and position of text and page elements on a page.

PDF (Portable Document Format). A file format created by Adobe Systems for document exchange.

PEs. Refers to "Printer Errors," but generally means errors by the typesetter, who may not be the printer.

POD (print-on-demand). Digital printing that enables copies to be made in small quantities.

ppi (pixels per inch). Sometimes equated with dpi (dots per inch) used in printing because both are used to measure resolution. Images and text can be printed at the same physical size (such as 3" × 5") and have different ppi counts, meaning an image can be the right physical size but have the wrong resolution. Most computer monitors display images at 72 ppi, but the same physical size image needs to be at least 300 ppi for process printing for clarity of image.

prepress production. Refers to the production necessary to get a project ready for printing, such as typesetting, page layout, and file preparation.

press check. The act of checking printed samples as they come off a printing press.

press-ready. Files that are ready to be printed and that will print without unexpected errors.

print run. The number of copies to be printed.

printer proofs. Required printed samples provided by a printer that demonstrate the likely outcome of the final printed product and that must be approved before printing can proceed. See also *wet proofs*, *digital proofs*, and *ozalids*.

process printing. Process printing sometimes involves generating film from files and printing plates from the film. In many cases today, the film is eliminated using direct-to-plate process printing, meaning the printing plate is produced directly from digital files with a computer. In either case, a full range of colors are printed from a configuration of small dots made with combinations of only four process inks—cyan, magenta, yellow and black. Also known as *offset* (when it uses film) and *direct-to-plate* printing (when it doesn't use film).

proofs. See *printer proofs*.

resolution. For Web and print, see *ppi*.

RGB. Optimum color model for Web and ebook images using the three additive colors red, green, and blue to create a wide array of colors.

rich black. 100% black printed together with a percentage of one or more process colors—sometimes 60% cyan, 40% magenta, 40% yellow. This allows the black to print much darker or richer than it would otherwise.

river. Formation of word spaces that together create the impression of a river of white on the text page. Considered undesirable.

royalty free. Type of contract or license agreement with a range of meanings, but most often stipulating that an image can be used for one fee in perpetuity and/or in certain contexts without paying additional royalties other than the initial fee.

running head. The book title, chapter title, or author name repeated at the top of each page.

saddle stitching. Binding method using wire staples through the middle fold. This method is sometimes used for books with very few pages.

signature. In process printing, a large single sheet of paper that when folded and trimmed comprises a section of pages in a book, usually numbering 16 pages. This means that the *total page count* in most process printed books must be divisible by 16. Color children's books, for example, are usually 32 pages in length (2 signatures of 16 pages).

slip case. A case or box for a book that displays the spine.

spine. The bound edge of the book.

spread. Two open facing pages.

stack. In typography, the undesirable coincidence of the same word appearing together at the end or beginning of two or more lines of the same text column.

style tag. A simple letter code or series of letters used to designate an element in a book that requires a specific style, such as <AH>, which signifies an A-head.

text column. A column of text on a page.

trim size. The finished size of the bound and trimmed pages of a printed book. A common U.S. paperback trim size is 6" × 9".

typesetting. The process of formatting text into specific font characteristics, such as styles and sizes.

URL (Uniform Resource Locator). Internet address. Different from a domain name in that it is the complete Internet address used to navigate to access those pages.

USP (unique selling proposition). Marketing term invented by Rosser Reeves that has come to mean the key characteristic or idea that differentiates one product from competing products.

Web site. A page or collection of pages and digital assets (images, text, videos, etc.) hosted on a server and made available on the Internet.

wet proofs. Proof made on press using the plates, ink, and paper specified for the project. Also referred to as *trial proofs*.

widow. Last line of a paragraph at the top of a page, or short one or two word line at the end of a paragraph. It is an undesirable copyfitting error that is to be avoided.

Index